UNDERSTANDING
Today's Adults

25 Years and Older

Jim Walter

LifeWay Press

Nashville, Tennessee

ISBN 0-6330-1379-X

Dewey Decimal Classification: 305.24

Subject Heading: ADULTS \ TEACHING

This book is a text for course number LS-0035

in the Adult Leadership Diploma Plan of the Christian Growth Study Plan.

Unless otherwise noted, all Scripture is from the Holy Bible, New International Version,

copyright © 1973, 1978, 1984 by International Bible Society.

Printed in the United States of America.

LifeWay Christian Resources

of the Southern Baptist Convention

127 Ninth Avenue, North

Nashville, Tennessee 37234

Contents

Have you ever sat on a bench at the mall just to watch and listen to people as they walk by? During a quiet moment of a worship service, have you looked around and considered how God created such a diverse universe of people? If so, you are well aware of how they differ from one another as well as how they are similar. If you have not stopped to observe the adults around you, take a few moments to do so during your next session with the adults you teach at church.

God has truly blessed you with the opportunity to teach adults during this time in history. You have a tremendous opportunity to let God work through you in their lives. If you are willing to let God minister through you, lives will be transformed and become more Christlike. You can make a difference in our world!

Why should you take the time to watch and listen to the men and women in your group? They are sending you messages and signals that help you understand the way God made them. God created each one of them in His image and to glorify Him. The more you understand them, the more you understand their Creator. In this sense, teaching adults is an act of worship that is pleasing to God.

In addition, God is teaching you how to teach adults. He has given you this opportunity as a gift with the promise to guide you to be the best teacher. That is what this book is about. It is designed to be a tool for teachers in understanding the needs that God gives all adults. This book is a collection of articles that provide insights in accepting and helping adults deal with various life situations. Through prayer God will help you understand each unique adult and his unique situation. With this understanding you can guide adults to apply the truth in God's Word to meet their needs and answer their problems. When adults connect their lives with the truth in God's Word, they can find the living Lord in their lives.

When you understand adults individually, the way God created them, you are truly able to let God use you in their lives. For example, when you accept that adults learn in a variety of ways, you will understand that you need to use a variety of approaches to learning. With this understanding carefully construct your teaching plan to include a variety of approaches instead of one approach. Consequently, effective teaching that leads people to our living Lord is a result of a positive understanding of the way God created men and women who live in today's world.

The Author

Dr. Jim Walter writes this resource from 31 years of experience in ministering with adults. Today he is the minister to median and senior adults at First Baptist Church, Pensacola, Florida. At the end of the Spring semester, 2000, Dr. Walter retired from a faculty position with Southwestern Baptist Theological Seminary in Fort Worth, Texas, after 14 years of teaching adult education.

Before going to the seminary to teach, Dr. Walter served as an Adult Sunday School consultant for the Sunday School Board (now LifeWay Christian Resources of the Southern Baptist Convention). During these 10 years, he traveled throughout the United States assisting teachers of adults to be effective in their ministries. He has also written numerous articles in periodicals including *Christian Single* and *Missions Today*.

In preparation for these ministries, Dr. Walter has served as minister with adults in churches in Texas and Florida. He received his M.R.E. in 1965 from Southwestern Baptist Theological Seminary, Ed.D. in 1968 from Tennessee State University (adult education), Ph.D. in 1994 from Southwestern Baptist Theological Seminary (religious education), Ed.D. in 1996 from the University of North Texas (adult education), and M.S. from the University of North Texas in Applied Gerontology.

On a personal note, Dr. Walter is married to Becky Lyn Vandenbark, and they have three sons, Steven, David, and John.

Appreciation

Many thanks to the group of Southern Baptist leaders of adults who designed and guided the development of this resource:

Jere Adams (LifeWay Christian Resources—Music)

Debra Berry (Woman's Missionary Union)

David Briscoe (LifeWay Christian Resources—Sunday School)

David Chamberlain (LifeWay Christian Resources—Marketing)

Michael Felder (LifeWay Christian Resources—Sunday School)

Brad Goad (LifeWay Christian Resources—Discipleship and Family)

Rick Howerton (LifeWay Christian Resources—Discipleship and Family)

Rich Murrell (LifeWay Christian Resources—Discipleship and Family)

Ron Pratt (LifeWay Christian Resources—Pastor-Staff Leadership)

Kathy Sharp (LifeWay Christian Resources—Magazines)

Sean Taylor (North American Mission Board—Mission Education)

Suggestions for Ways to Use This Resource

As you read and study each article, consider the adults in your group. You will not find pictures in this resource because we want to provide you with an inexpensive tool for developing your teaching skills. We also want you to think of the adults in your group. To enhance your experience with this book, take pictures of the men and women in your group as a group, then individually. Lay the pictures on the table nearby as you read the articles. Or tape them to your computer.

As you read an article, apply the discussion to each person. How does the information relate to him or her? Use the discussion to prompt a desire to know more about each person. As you reflect on each article, answer the "AdultApplication" questions by taking notes on how the information applies to each specific person in your group. The more you understand each person, the more effective you will be in guiding him or her to our living Lord.

You have choices as to how you will engage this resource.

1. **Online:** click on *www.lifeway.com/bibleinsites/understanding.asp* for a free online guide of this resource.

2. **Download:** click on *www.lifeway.com/bibleinsites/understanding.asp* to download the resource at no cost. You are welcome to make copies for others in your church or school. Or print out specific articles as you need them.

3. **Text:** A text is available for $5.95 plus shipping. Call 1-800-458-2772 to order. Please allow three weeks for printing and shipping.

Leadership Development Resource Series

This resource is part of a series of resources designed to equip teachers of adults as they let God use them in the lives of their students. The information you will explore in this resource answers the *who* and *why* questions. Whom do we teach? Why do we teach the way we do? The **what** question will always be answered with the Bible. The Bible guides us in becoming Christlike in all that we do and say. It is our source of information that leads us to our living Lord.

If you minister with all adults, you are encouraged to use the companion resource related to young adults titled ***Developing Tomorrow's Leaders Today: Understanding Young Adults 18–24 Years***. In addition, the following resources answer the "how to teach" question. You will also find administration resources that answer the when and where questions. All of these resources are available by calling 1-800-458-2772 or online at *www.lifewaystores.com*:

Adults on Mission℠

Adults on Mission Guide

Teaching Adults: A Guide for Transformational Teaching

Baptist Men on Mission

Leading Baptist Men on Mission Manual

Teaching Adults: A Guide for Transformational Teaching

Discipleship Training

Transformational Discipleship: Your Church Helping People Be like Jesus

Teaching Adults: A Guide for Transformational Teaching

Share Jesus Without Fear

Family Ministry

How to Minister to Families in Your Church (available 3/1/01)

Teaching Adults: A Guide for Transformational Teaching

Witnessing Through Your Relationships

Men's Ministry

Drawing Men to God: Men's Ministry Manual

Teaching Adults: A Guide for Transformational Teaching

Jesus on Leadership: Becoming a Servant Leader

Music Ministry

Senior Adult Choir Ministry: Age Is No Excuse

Senior Adult Ministry

Forward Together: A New Vision for Senior Adult Ministry

Teaching Adults: A Guide for Transformational Teaching

Single Adult Ministry

The Single Adult Ministry Solution

Teaching Adults: A Guide for Transformational Teaching

Witnessing Through Your Relationships

Sunday School

Adult Sunday School for a New Century

Teaching Adults: A Guide for Transformational Teaching

*A Place for Everyone: A Guide for Special Education Bible
    Teaching-Reaching Ministry*

Women on Mission®

Women on Mission Guide

Five Steps to the Great Commission

Teaching Adults: A Guide for Transformational Teaching

Women's Enrichment Ministry

Transformed Lives: Taking Women's Ministry to the Next Level

Teaching Adults: A Guide for Transformational Teaching

WiseCounsel: Skill for Lay Counseling—LIFE Course

What Does It Mean to Be an Adult?

When did you first discover you were an adult? Was it the first time you were addressed as "Sir" or "Ma'am"? Was it when you and your mate brought your newborn home from the hospital? Was it when you no longer relied on your parents for at least part of your livelihood?

What are some of the signs of being an adult? Most of us think of the physical signs, but there are other signs as well—moving into a business position you have long desired, taking on the management of a household, sharing deep thoughts with one's spouse, taking a strong interest in civic affairs. The list could go on and on. Clearly, adulthood is different from childhood and youth.

Again, what does it mean to be an adult? We attach unusual names to lifestyles among adults:

YUPPIES—young, urban professionals

SIPPIES—senior, independent professionals

YUMMIES—young, upwardly mobile ministers

WOOPIES—well-off older people

DUMPIES—destitute, unprepared middle-age people

DINKS—dual income, no kids

One indication of the tawdry nature of adulthood in our day is TV and motion picture parental guidelines. For instance, TVPG means that the film or program may contain some material parents would find unsuitable for young children. It may contain occasional coarse language, limited violence, and some suggestive sexual dialogue.

Even stronger is the designation TVM or R rating. These programs and films are specifically targeted to adults and are unsuited for children under 17. These shows have "mature" themes, profane language, and graphic violence.

In our society the word adult is frequently associated with pornography, as in "adult situations" and "adult videos." Here the word *adult* has a double meaning. It acts as a warning to those who guard the entertainment choices of children and youth. It also advertises commercial sleaze to those who want provocative depictions of the human condition. Those who provide such programs know how to appeal to those who want explicit sex and violence. But the meaning of sex and violence goes much deeper. When these films are associated with the word *adult,* they convey to children and youth that these are appropriate subject matter for adults but not for them. That is, only (mature) adults can watch such material. Kids pick up on the signals. They begin to associate "adult" language with situational exploration as a part of adult behavior. That is, it is something they can look forward to, something that defines expected adult behavior.

What then is the Christian response? Followers of Jesus must give their children and youth a better definition of adulthood. The word *adult* must be cleansed of its vulgarity. Mature should reflect a sense of responsibility, of sound judgment, of caring purpose. Only when children and youth can look forward to moral living in adulthood can we again associate adulthood with maturity.

AdultApplication: When did you first see yourself as an adult? If mature behavior defines being an adult, what characteristics and life situations do you see in yourself or your class members that would indicate that you or they are adults? If it were your responsibility, or your class's, to model adult behavior for children and youth in your church, what behaviors would you like to change? Is such modeling your responsibility? Is it ultimately the responsibility of all Christian adults?

_____

_____

_____

_____

Stereotyping Adults

Several years ago I taught a Sunday School class of couples in their thirties. Among the regular attendees were two couples, one from India and the other second-generation Chinese. One Sunday we combined our class with an older couples class because the lesson was on old age. After the class a member of the older class came up to me and started talking about how good it was to have "foreigners" in our class today and how they contributed to the discussion. I smiled in response but later thought to myself, *Why did he single out one identifying characteristic and focus on that for his conversation? Was he surprised that they could hold their own in the discussion, considering that they were not Anglos? Were the color of their skin and their facial features all he could recognize about them?*

Prejudicial people look for differences between people. They focus discussion and conversation on these unique features. More than five hundred years ago John Donne gave a singular expression to this idea that all of us are part of a unity, the human race. He wrote, "No man is an island, entire of itself; every man is a piece of the continent, a part of the main; if a clod be washed away by the sea, Europe is the less . . . ; any man's death diminishes me, because I am involved in mankind." We are all in this together, in the streets of Kosovo, the rural villages of the Australian outback, the great cities of the United States, or the countryside of Missouri or Ohio. The Hakka of China, the Chechen of southern Russia, the Somali of northeast Africa, the Sudanese of Indonesia are all part of our life together.

AdultApplication: Think about this. How do stereotypes of people get in the way of knowing adults as people? In your church what stereotypes fit in easily? What stereotypes would quickly be excluded?

Adult education in the church is an enigma, a seeming contradiction. Why? Hazel Rodgers, late veteran Adult Sunday School leader, listed several statements that describe

reasons churches do not take up the adult challenge. Think about your church. Record your response to each of these statements. Where does your church need to improve its provision and priority on ministry with adults?

• **Churches typically ignore the adult population.**

_____

_____

_____

• **Churches largely disregard the biblical focus on adults.**

_____

_____

_____

• **Churches generally write off the adult population.**

_____

_____

_____

• **Churches usually have no strategy for reaching adults.**

_____

• **Churches routinely fail to update their adult organizations.**

• **Churches ordinarily believe that adult evangelism is only a secondary matter.**

• **Churches manifestly cannot expect adults to respond to them while these negative attitudes prevail.**

Twenty-first Century Demographics of Adults

Increasingly throughout the world people face the prospect of living far more than "three score and ten." And still there is more news about the changing family. Married couples are a bare majority of U.S. households. Only about one-third of households have any children under 18 present. People who live alone comprise one-fourth of U.S. households.

Do you want to live to be a hundred years old? Already the fastest growing age group is 90 plus, and as might be inferred from this discussion, the median age of the population is growing older. In 1990, it was 33 years; in 1995, it moved up to 34.7; and in 2000, it is 36.4. The non-Hispanic white population in the U.S. will decline to 67.6 percent, and minority populations will increase to 13.2 percent African-American; 13.2 percent Hispanic; 5.9 Asian; and 0.9 percent Native American, Eskimo, and Aleutian. By the middle of this century, it is projected that the United States population will be one-half non-Hispanic white and moving toward a majority that is currently a minority.

Christian leaders of adults must face the demographic realities at the beginning of this new millennium. Consider these facts:

- In 2010, just a few years away, there will be 2.9 workers for every person receiving Social Security. In 1950, there were 16.6 workers for every person receiving Social Security.
- In 2010, a "1997 dollar" will be worth about 63 cents.
- In 2000, your chance of contracting malignant melanoma is 1 in 75. In 1935, the risk was 1 in 1,500.
- Shortly after 2020, there will be more Americans over age 65 than under age 13.
- Not surprisingly, there will be a drop in the number of persons in the 25–34 category, while adults 45–54 will realize a dramatic growth. The 1990 Census reveals that 33 states had fewer youth in 1990 than they did in 1980.
- The youngest baby boomers—those born between 1956 and 1964 are moving out of their childbearing years.

• Furthermore, 70 million baby boomers are lifetime learners.

• And youth account for only 16 percent of the population.

Already apparent is an enormous growth in the number of older persons in our nation. Revolutionary changes in society call for revolutionary thinking and innovative solutions. Aging must be viewed as a lifelong and society-wide process, not just a phenomenon affecting older adults. As an example, older persons will become more involved in civic life than their parents. People will live longer and have several careers. Already government agencies classify elderly status as age 62 or older, rather than 65. Coincidentally, that is the average retirement age.

The Census Bureau reports that the number of older Americans is growing faster than other segments of the population. The preeminent fact about the elderly population is its size and comparatively rapid growth: There were 34.1 million people age 65 years or older in the United States in 1997. One in 8 Americans is a senior citizen today, compared to only 1 in 25 at the dawn of the last century.

The number of older Americans has increased by more than 9 percent since 1990, compared with a rise of 7 percent among persons under age 65. And this disparity is occurring at a low ebb in elderly population growth. Men and women reaching age 65 today were born during the Great Depression, when birthrates were particularly low. This relative pause in elderly population increases will end abruptly around 2010, when those born during the post-World War II baby boom begin to retire. Today's elderly population is expected to double by 2030, expanding at a rate of almost 3 percent each year to almost 70 million people. The Census Bureau estimates that 20 percent of Americans will be older than retirement age in 2030, compared with less than 13 percent today. These demographic trends merit further examination.

• The largest and fastest growing segments of the older population include many people who have historically been vulnerable economically: women, minorities, and the "oldest old." This explosive growth sends a straightforward message to our churches and church leaders: more and more of our church buildings, church budgets, staff member's time and creativity should be devoted to seniors and their needs and potential. However this begs the further question: which subgroups of seniors need this special attention?

• The ranks of the oldest Americans—those 85 years old and over—are swelling much more rapidly than those of the "young" elderly are. These oldest Americans made up less than 9 percent of the elderly population in 1980; they have grown to more than 11 percent of the elderly today and may make up 23 percent by 2050. As a consequence church leaders, members of building committees, and others need to know about special building considerations for the elderly. For instance, older persons with sight problems need increased lighting.

• Elderly women greatly outnumber men, particularly as they age. Women can expect to live 19 years after reaching age 65, compared to 15.8 years for men. In 1997, there were 143 elderly women for every 100 elderly men. For the oldest old (85 plus) the ratio grows to 248 women for every 100 men.

• Finally, more of America's seniors are minorities. Racial and ethnic minorities are younger on average than whites and have significantly lower life expectancies; nevertheless, their representation in the elderly population is increasing. In 1997, 15 percent of the U.S. elderly population were minorities; 8 percent were African-American. By 2025, 24 percent will be minorities.

Is there a connection between these demographics and your church? Yes. These trends reflect the statistical study of the population with regard to their size and density. In other words, the trends in the United States likely also reflect similar trends in your community, your church field, and the adults in your church who are 46–53, both members and prospects. Demographic studies provide valuable information.

Christian leaders should know about adults in general, about their age, level of education, how many people are in a household and who they are, their income group, their employment status, and many other distinctives. If, for instance, you are teaching a Sunday School class of persons 46–53, you will need to know pertinent information about them. It is not enough for teachers to know their subject matter well; they must also know about the people in the class. Part of the blame for ineffective lessons or classroom studies can be laid on teachers who have studied their lesson well but cannot relate lesson content to the real needs of participants. They have understudied members and perhaps have overstudied their lesson.

Of course, teachers assume they know their participants based on their experiences together at church. Unfortunately, adults often do not project their needs honestly in church. In fact, an adult can easily appear to be one kind of person at church but a different kind of person the rest of the time. We can gain some information from church experiences, but that is no match for knowing each person one-on-one in personal visits and other engagements.

One value of demographic studies about the church community is that church leaders can match the ministries of the church more closely to those whom they are called to serve. One church had a long history of Anglo ministers. The church field began to change to an older, Hispanic neighborhood in the 70s, yet the church still retained the same staff composition. A new pastor came onto the field in 1998, looked at the field, and found them not "white" unto harvest but brown and black. He looked at adults in general—their ages, levels of education, the number of people in a typical household and who they were, their income groups, their employment status, and many other distinctives. With this information and the guidance of a church growth task force, the church decided to call a Hispanic minister of music and senior adults. This combination took some adjustment for the congregation, but in the past year they have seen a number of Hispanics join the previously all-Anglo church. One is now a deacon.

In another case, Calvary Baptist Church recognized that their building allocations did not match the new demographics of the 21st century. In the 60s, they had a large youth group and built their present building accordingly. Now they have fewer youth and children, but the adult population the church is called to reach can barely fit into the two department rooms, which were sufficient 30 years ago. What will they do? In the next few years they plan to convert youth and children's space into adult rooms to provide for the needed and anticipated growth in adults, particularly senior adults. On the drawing board are six adult departments instead of the current two.

For further reading on adult development, consult Helen Bee and Barbara Bjorklaund, *The Journey of Adulthood,* Fourth Edition (Upper Saddle River, NJ: Prentice Hall, 2000).

AdultApplication: **What do these statistics say to churches planning to build in the next 20 years? What modifications would your building require to meet the needs of a growing adult population? How would your church ministries need to change? Will staff assignments need to be adjusted? Are your church leaders preparing for this new demographic reality?**

_____

_____

_____

_____

_____

_____

_____

Adult Development

Analyzing adults in this generation means that we must be perceptive in understanding them. In recent years we have seen many paradigms describing adulthood. Actually, the journey of adulthood has a rich and colorful past, and most of the serious research has been done in the 20th century. As we study the adult journey, let's pause and describe what we mean by adult *development.*

We say that flowers develop from bulbs, that Maria took a roll of film to be developed, that Ron is developing a cold. Obviously all development means change, but not all change is developmental. For instance, if we change from an older small car to a sports utility vehicle (and incur a $37,000 debt!), it is a change but hardly a sign of development. (Some of you would challenge that statement!)

Change is inevitable and continual. But more pertinent to this discussion is the idea of development. Development is coherent and organized, somewhat predictable, and progresses from simple to complex. Obviously, the adults in your group want to develop, not just change. In the spiritual arena the term *development* means "getting better." Persons grow through learning experiences and because of maturation. People develop throughout their life span.

The interaction of maturation and experience varies as we grow older. In childhood and youth years maturation plays a more significant role. Adult experience begins to play a more important role. For instance, a small child cannot manipulate today's multifaceted remote controls, but adults quickly gain expertise in flipping channels. In Christian education one must truly believe that older adults should continue to develop, regardless of their physical condition.

Another way to describe adult growth is by age- and history-graded influences. In adulthood, age-graded influences include biological influences such as menopause and diminished sexual potency. They also include cultural events such as retirement, marriage, and the choice to remain single. On the other hand, history-graded events such as the worldwide depression of the 30s, the Vietnam War, the GI bill, and the introduction of Medicare in 1965. These events affect persons differently. For instance, the explosion at the Three Mile Island nuclear plant in eastern Pennsylvania did not affect me. However, the rise and eventual fall of the Texas economy in the 1980s did affect my family and me. History-graded events also include such cultural developments as computers, television, and the changing roles for women.

Finally, nonnormative life events are unusual events that have a major impact on people. For instance, a man remarries following widowhood and becomes a father at 55, or a woman has great success in her business and retires at 40 to spend the rest of her life as a volunteer chaplain at a woman's prison. Such events, whether negative or positive, can cause stress if a person has not prepared for these events or has to have special help in adapting.

AdultApplication: Using an approach to understanding adulthood based on age and history is both comprehensible and flexible. Which age and historical events have shaped you? What kinds of events have shaped members of your class? Were events normative or atypical? Were they expected or unexpected? How do these influences on your life influence your participation in adult Christian education?

_____

_____

_____

_____

_____

_____

The Primary Needs of Adults

Throughout the ministry of Jesus, He started teaching by meeting needs of His learners. With the woman at the well, He started with her need for water (John 4:7-26). With Zaccheus, He invited him to come down from the tree so that he could see and hear Jesus (Luke 19:1-10). With the centurion, Jesus healed the servant (Luke 7:1-10). The same approach of meeting needs through Bible study and discipleship opportunities is effective for leaders today. By first addressing the needs of adults, leaders and teachers are helping adults find how God meets their needs through the Bible. Only then do Bible study and discipleship become relevant to their everyday lives.

Gilbert Peterson identified six primary needs of adults in his book *The Christian Education of Adults.* All adults in some form experience these needs: physical, security, affection, significance, accomplishment, and creativity. With these in mind, ministry leaders and teachers can plan Bible studies, discipleship opportunities, and ministry/missions avenues that will address these needs and allow God to work in the lives of adults.

Physical Needs

Human beings of all ages need sleep, food, water, air, and exercise. These needs stem from bodily functions. Adults, however, experience physical changes that affect how these needs are met in their lives.

During midlife, men experience a decrease in their physical strength. Kenneth Gangel and James Wilhoit pointed out in their book, *The Christian Educator's Handbook on Adult Education,* that this decline involves their ability to learn and perform large psychomotor skills. This decline initiates a need to change eating habits and exercise regimen. Women experience menopause during midlife. This physical change affects sleep patterns. Many women adjust their eating and exercise habits to combat their spreading waistlines.

In addition, many adults struggle with other types of physical declines. A loss of hearing ability, particularly with high-pitched tones, is common among both men and women. A sharp decline in visual acuity causes many adults to wear glasses or contact lenses. The metabolism of their bodies begins to slow down, which causes weight problems for most adults. In a more serious concern, Jerry Stubblefield, professor of Christian education at Golden Gate Baptist Theological Seminary, wrote in his book *A Church Ministering to Adults* that after the onset of the 40s, the heart, lungs, kidneys, and liver begin to malfunction.

Concern for health becomes an issue for most adults during the middle years. Anxiety over health concerns can cause adults to be open to ministry that is intended to help them deal with their anxiety. Churches are wise to be sensitive to these health concerns.

Security

The need for security is a common need for preschoolers, children, youth, and adults. Security is feeling safe physically and emotionally. It also involves a feeling of acceptance by others. Acceptance by Jesus Christ is a spiritual experience that meets the need for security. The doctrine of the security of the believer confirms that Christ's acceptance is eternal. It can never be taken away. This spiritual security is an important gift to all adults.

In his book *Foundations of Ministry,* Michael Anthony warned church leaders to avoid assuming that all Christian adults have a personal relationship with Jesus Christ. Churches are full of adult believers who have accepted Jesus Christ as their Savior but have never become His disciples. They may never have experienced Christ's acceptance. In George Barna's "State of the Church, 2000" report, he concluded that half of the people who say they are born again have lost souls (Ted Byfield and Virginia Byfield, "Half the Born-Agains are Still Lost Souls, a Researcher Finds, and There's a Reason," *Report/Newsmagazine,* 27:9 [9/11/2000]: 54). Bible study, discipleship opportunities, and missions education have the potential of helping adults experience Christ's acceptance and be transformed by His love.

In addition to experiencing spiritual security, physical changes in adulthood affect the level of security for both men and women. Men express heightened concerns over their physical health. Women fear that the changes in their physical appearance will decrease their ability to be attractive and interesting.

Consequently, physical changes promote the need for security in adulthood.

In regard to goals in life, midlife brings feelings of insecurity. Men often struggle with goals and values, which may cause them to experience a sense of failure. Underemployment is a concern for many men. Women also struggle with goals and values, but their struggle differs from that of men. Most women in midlife have never had goals. They struggle with a shift from inside the home to outside the family as their children leave home. These struggles can be diminished by an internal sense of security.

The stereotypes of adults often cause confusion among adults themselves. They equate stability with maturity. They think they are supposed to be controlled and restrained in their outlook. However, they often find themselves "seething with anxiety" (Charles M. Sell, *Transitions Through Adult Life* [Grand Rapids: Zondervan Publishing House, 1991], 133). By accepting these anxious feelings, adults can retain their sense of security. Christian education can meet this need of security by providing small-group opportunities where adults can talk about their struggles. They can share ways to understand what is happening and accept one another with love.

Hence, the crises of life may cause adults to become involved in learning activities. Through these learning activities they are attempting to meet their need for security. By understanding their situations and experiences, they can accept what is happening to them as normal and respond with a feeling of security. One way to meet physical needs is to provide the *fit4 Wellness Plan* as a small-group opportunity (available by calling 1-800-458-2772).

Affection

Peterson also identified the need for affection as a specific concern for middle and older adults that may or may not be a specific need for young adults. As a result of the major physical changes taking place in midlife, affection becomes an important need that must be met.

A transition that prompts the need for affection is the departure of children from the home. The empty-nest experience influences the number of friends. As children mature and leave home, parents find themselves searching for the affection they once received from their children. Their number of social contacts may diminish as their children graduate from high school. They no longer have social contacts stemming from the their children's activities. Again, small-group opportunities for parents can meet the need for affection.

As adults have fewer friends, the quality of these relationships become more intense and significant than in young adulthood. Friends are no longer just people with whom to socialize on the weekends; they become sources of support and companionship as they experience life crises together. The affection they share for one another becomes a source of strength and encouragement.

Adults experiencing special circumstances also heighten the need for affection. Divorce, underemployment, unemployment, health problems, and death of family members become common experiences of the adult years. Expressions of affection can help adults journey through the grief associated with these experiences.

Significance

Another basic need of all adults is a sense of significance. It is feeling appreciated by others. This need is particularly important to middle adults because of the way they are pressed into service by family, church, and community.

One tends to find a sense of inadequacy with a self-perspective largely reflected by roles played as a spouse, parent, and employee. These feelings of inadequacy play a role in the intensity of a person's midlife crisis. However, part of the results of the transitions taking place in midlife is the opportunity for renewal and authenticity. Both men and women in midlife find their identity as someone's spouse or parent to be satisfying. As their need for significance is met, they develop an authentic self-worth based on themselves, not someone else.

As Christians, however, the need for significance was met in creation. The fact that human beings are created in God's image and by His love is truly grounds for significance (Gen. 1:27). As children of God, believers find their self- human need for recognition or appreciation is part of what it means to be made in God's image. God needs human beings to thank Him for all of His blessings. In a similar way human beings need worth in God's love.

Recognition for one's accomplishments is important. Adults desire forms of recognition that suit their personalities. For example, a shy person would not want to be recognized in front of a group. Whether they receive recognition greatly affects their sense of self-worth. This external source of self-worth can result in frustration. When a sense of self-worth is anchored in God's love, adults can accept appreciation from others with a healthy sense of significance.

Accomplishment

A fifth primary need of adults is accomplishment. Whether adults are home-makers, firefighters, engineers, teachers, or artists, God creates human beings with a drive to accomplish something during their lives.

Despite some physical decline, most adults do not experience intellectual decline. In midlife, adults often pursue goals that involve mental skills such as academic degrees. In *Adult Development and Learning,* Alan Knox identified the following major characteristics of home and family settings that contribute to accomplishment in life:

- Acceptance by family members that adult life entails growth and change.
- Familiarity with other adults as role models engaged in systematic learning and adaptation.
- Availability of learning resources for adults in the home, such as books, recordings, and study guides.
- Awareness of opportunities for organized learning outside the home.
- Opportunities for activities that clarify needs to grow and change.
- Willingness for adult members to spend time and money on continuing their education, along with encouragement and recognition when they do.

Christian education can play an important role in meeting the need for accomplishment. In *The Adult Learning Projects,* Allen Tough noted that adults prefer learning self-directed opportunities where teachers serve as facilitators. As they learn this way, they experience accomplishment. As teachers, they need guidance in developing their teaching skills that allows them to be self-directed and recognizes their accomplishments. They need opportunities to discuss and reflect on their experiences with a small group of fellow teachers. The Christian Growth Study Plan (*www.lifeway.com/cgsp/catalog* or call 1-800-968-5519) can be a learning strategy for adults to pursue on their own and receive recognition when they accomplish or complete courses. Church leaders are wise to provide these kinds of opportunities for the adults in their churches.

Creativity

The final primary need of adults identified by Peterson is creativity. Just as God is creative, adults are open to creative change in their lives. During the adult years, the need for creativity is met by opportunities for new experiences. These new experiences may stem from the physical changes for men and women. A red sports car may meet a man's need for creativity when he experiences a receding hairline or expanding waistline. A home-based business may meet a woman's need for creativity when her child-rearing duties end.

The need for creativity is also met by new relationships. For most, these new friendships are healthy expressions of creativity for both men and women. Again, church families can provide a variety of fellowship opportunities for adults who need healthy relationships with Christian friends.

Adults also need to be creative. Drama, art, music, and even teaching Bible studies can give adults the opportunities to use their skills and talents in creative ways. These opportunities can be strategic side doors for many secular persons to enter the church. They can get to know people in a church family and develop relationships that can eventually bring them to Jesus Christ.

AdultApplication: As you reflect on these needs of adults, identify how you experience these needs. This identification will help you relate to the adults in your group.

How can you meet the needs of the adults in your group?

_____

_____

Written by Morlee Maynard, ministry coordination specialist, LifeWay Church Resources.

The Real Middle Adult

As mentioned earlier, American society is facing an emerging majority of persons in the late forties and early fifties. David Karp, in *The Gerontologist,* conducted a study to discover the commonalties of women and men aged 50 to 60 years. He found that the fifties were a time in which the "pace of aging messages greatly increases and picks up momentum. . . .The fifties is a kind of fulcrum decade, a turning point in the aging process, during which people, more sharply than before, are made to feel their age. As the fifties progress, it becomes harder to avoid the recognition of really growing older. Particular events occur, such as the deaths of parents and friends, being in the middle of three generations, being the oldest at work, and becoming grandparents, which make aging a prominent part of self-consciousness in the fifties. For this reason, the fifties can be characterized as a decade of reminders."

AdultApplication: **Read that paragraph again. List your church members who are in their fifties and indicate circumstances which are similar to this description.**

_____

_____

_____

_____

The Empty Nest

The growing number of middle-age persons, that is, persons between age 40 and 60 has issued a new set of issues, problems, and benefits. One issue many middle adults face is the prospect and process of the "empty nest," when the children leave home. Does this happen to all families? How does children's leaving the home affect the middle-age marriage? How can the Christian couple improve their marital relationship in the years ahead?

People are living longer and can look forward to many more years after their children leave home. In the early part of the last century, women were expected to live into their forties and fifties. Now many women can look forward to living well into their 80s. Even the term *middle age* is a modern phenomenon. Children leave behind parents who are functional and vital.

The term *empty nest syndrome* refers to the time of adjustment for parents when their children leave home, especially when their last child leaves home. It is typically associated with stress, grief, anxiety, identity crisis, and heartache. This is especially true for mothers because they are the emotional caretakers of the household. For some this is a major crisis. All of a sudden her role has changed. One woman said, "When our last daughter leaves for college on Thursday, I don't know what I will do. I know it's best for her, but I will miss her desperately around the house. I almost feel my life is over."

What about the term *empty nest*? Some would suggest that the term should be discarded. It means to them that women are chickens or birds, or worse, old hens. This is blatant sexism or ageism. Another term is *post-parental,* a term indicating that the role of parenting loses its importance and is a more accurate indicator of the second half of life. An alternative term is *mother emeritus,* a term that maintains the honor motherhood deserves but indicates that some of the parenthood tasks have ended.

The question arises, does the empty next exist? Some have argued that it doesn't. Most women do not get depressed *after* the children leave home but when they *don't* leave home. This is called the unemptied nest. Or, more humorously, the middle-age crisis! Another term is the *boomerang children,* those young adults who, having left, return home to live.

On the other hand women report that raising teenagers is certainly stressful, and after the children leave home, they experience an increased sense of well-being, freedom, privacy, and relief from parenting responsibilities. This may be related to the changing role of women in society. Many women shift to a career mindset. Women of ethnic minority cultures have strong ties with their extended families, which give them support. Any negative effects of this period of middle age may be due to the general effects of aging or an unsatisfying marital relationship, not because the children have left the home. One way couples have overcome any negatives of the empty nest is through beginning or intensifying their intimacy after the children leave home.

Rediscovering Intimacy in the Middle Years

The institution of marriage is becoming one of the most volatile and temporary institutions of today's society. God created marriage to meet the needs of women and men, yet in many marriages just the opposite is happening. What was created to bring pleasure and fulfillment is often the primary cause of strife and heartache. One of the most intense longings of the human heart is to love and be loved. And the security of marriage offers Christian couples one of the ultimate pleasures of life and heals loneliness as nothing else can.

The word *intimate* comes from a Latin word meaning "inmost." It is associated as closeness and rapport with another, as mutuality and compatibility. According to these descriptions, single persons can enjoy intimacy as well. In fact, unless a single person can become intimate with another person before marriage, he or she is not ready for marriage. Unfortunately most people equate intimacy with a sexual experience. Intimacy is the only proper foundation for expressing sexuality in marriage for the Christian married couple. Without intimacy sex becomes only marital recreation, devoid of love.

God intends for His creation to have intimacy with others. He created people to be close to one another. "The LORD God said, 'It is not good for the man to be alone. I will make a helper suitable for him" (Gen. 2:18). This passage teaches us that Adam's closeness to God did not erase his need for human companionship. God does not replace human companionship. He creates us to have a relationship with Him. He also creates men and women to have an intimate relationship with one another. This intimate relationship will help Christian couples ward off loneliness. "For this reason a man will leave his father and mother and be united to his wife, and they will become one flesh" (Gen. 2:24). "Without intimacy, a person feels isolated and unattached. This loneliness can be one of the most harrowing states of mind an individual can experience. It is like living in a shell" (Charles M. Sell, *Intimacy,* Multnomah Press, 1983).

Intimacy is not optional in marriage. Instead it is a necessary ingredient to keep the union healthy. Intimacy does not just involve the physical part of marriage, which is the first thing that occurs to many people when it is discussed. When a person, married or single, enters into intimacy, he or she walks into another's life—emotionally, socially, physically, and intellectually. "Shared privacy" is another definition.

AdultApplication: What difficulties do couples face when they decide to discuss the quality of their marriage?

_____

_____

_____

As strange as it may seem, the answer to better intimacy in the middle years is not for a couple to plan to be more intimate. The answer lies in a couple's dealing forthrightly with anger. David Mace suggests that responsible understanding of anger is the first step in creating intimate relationships, both inside and outside of marriage.

The enemy of couple intimacy is not apathy but anger. We have two choices when we are angry with our spouse: ventilation or repression. Both seem like legitimate responses to deal with danger. Couples who use ventilation may strike their spouse or child or spew out profanity. Ugly newspaper head-lines every day show evidence of couples who fight each other to ventilate anger. More subtle, though, are couples who repress their anger. These men and women know that ventilation of anger is wrong, but instead of dealing responsibly with their anger, they hide or repress it.

Another approach is denial. People in denial about their anger rationalize that they can dispose of their anger much like taking out the garbage, and so they ignore it. What happens when two persons who ostensibly love each other do not opt for fighting but instead repress their anger? What happens when anger between couples is "bottled up"? Does it go away? No. When anger is continuously repressed, it turns into a low, simmering boil. It never goes away. We call this resentment. It may lead to psychosomatic illnesses. Of course, when one or both marriage partners repress their anger, they are driven away from each other, sometimes emotionally, sometimes physically. They lose the tenderness that strengthens marriage. The inner core of trust begins to disappear even though the couple maintains the appearance of affection and happiness. What are couples to do? Couples in this dilemma feel that repression is the only sensible alternative to a pitched battle. There is a solution.

Christian couples can move out from this quandary by first admitting their anger to each other. Just as a person may say, "I am hungry," or, "I feel tired," he or she can communicate, "I feel angry." Once this act honestly opens up communication, the second step is to pledge not to attack the other person. Too much is at stake to resort to physical violence. The third step in dealing with anger is for each of the partners to take responsibility for dealing with it. Husbands and wives realize that their marriage is more important than this incident of anger. When people become angry, their feelings are hurt, and their self-esteem is threatened. Focusing on the causes, rather than the anger itself, is the way couples can resolve their anger and regain intimacy.   When a marriage ends in divorce or a family breaks down, the failure always takes place from the inside. The generally supposed causes of marital trouble—difficulties with sex, money, in-laws, and child raising—are not the real causes. These are only the arenas in which the inner failure of the relationship is outwardly demonstrated. The inner failure of a close relationship always takes place for the same reason—because the persons involved have been unable to achieve mutual love and intimacy. The failure to achieve love and intimacy is almost always due to the inability of the persons concerned to deal creatively with anger.

AdultApplication: How can Bible study and discipleship groups be such a refuge for adults needing shared privacy?

_____

_____

_____

_____

How do married couples find intimacy? It is a private relationship all the defenses are removed. Spouses make themselves vulnerable with each other. No married couple really knows what marriage at its best can mean until they have done that with each other.

Physical intimacy is God's wedding present to a married couple. As a gift it is to be used with care and caution. A sexual union has everything to do with the relationship behind the act and little to do with physical skills. Several years ago I noticed the title of a book that aptly describes this intimate union: *Thank God for Sex!* While sex is easy, building a marriage with the ingredients of love, trust, tenderness, and unselfishness takes hard work and patience. Husbands and wives should not confine their expression of intimacy to a sexual union alone. They have a lifetime to experience many ways of expressing intimacy. Sexual intimacy is just one way.

Most couples would admit that their deepest expectation for marriage is not just love but intimacy. In the midst of a busy, uncaring, competitive world, everyone needs to have a chance to be deeply loved and fully known.

Ideas for Supporting Families in the Middle Years

How can churches and the Christian faith help parents face these critical years of post-parenthood?

Most church youth programs recognize high school seniors in May. But few focus on ministry to their parents who now face years without children at home. Have a seminar in the afternoon or evening just for the parents of these graduating seniors. Some topics you may explore are: improving your marriage, adjusting to the adult status of your children, creative financing for college costs, developing an adult faith, and finding fulfillment in ministry and missions. Allow ample time for participants to ask questions and share solutions. For further suggestions, use the resource *Transitions: Preparing for College* by Art Herron (Nashville: LifeWay Church Resources).

In preparing for Bible study, look for incidents in the middle years of biblical personalities. Most of the persons mentioned in the Bible are adults, many in their middle years. Develop specific programs to meet the distinctive needs of these prime timers. As needed, form support groups for grandparents raising grandchildren, aging parents, and other groups. Promote mission activities for these persons, which may include building a house for Habit for Humanity, lay renewal, or short-term overseas mission assignments.

AdultApplication: Look through popular magazines for advertisements that focus on interests of middle-age persons. Some examples are prescription drugs, house furnishings, makeup, and products to enhance beauty for men and women. List the life qualities these products promise.

Do men and women look at the middle years differently? If so, how?

_____

_____

_____

_____

It's Not Easy Being a Single Parent

Today in America one out of four children is being raised by a single parent. For the most part, single parenthood is the result of a divorce; however there are other possibilities such as single-parent adoption, births out of wedlock, widowhood, and separation of marital partners. Divorce, and attendant single parenthood, is not a respecter of persons. Divorce happens to the nicest persons! This article focuses on the special challenges single parents face as the result of divorce.

Take a quick quiz on single parenthood. Are these statements true or false? And, more importantly, why do you believe them to be so?

T / F   1. Children should be told when a divorce is imminent.

T / F   2. Children should be told all the shoddy details of the divorce.

T / F   3. Children should share the blame for the divorce.

T / F   4. Children should be made to decide with whom to live.

T / F   5. It is not necessary to reassure the children that both parents in divorce love them.

T / F   6. A child's right to be angry with you must be accepted.

T / F   7. It is best to change a child's environment soon after a divorce.

T / F   8. Your ability to cope with the pain of divorce has no affect on the child.

T / F   9. It is not necessary for you to cooperate in the children's visitation rights with your ex-spouse.

T / F   10. Professional help may be necessary for your children to adjust to the divorce.

(Answers: 1 T, 2 F, 3 F, 4 F, 5 F, 6 T, 7 F, 8 F, 9 F, 10 T)

Economic Concerns of Single Parents

Single-parent families headed by mothers are the poorest of all major demographic groups. The economic position of these parents has declined in recent years in comparison to the aged and disabled. These families are subject to new economic realities: income loss, loss of home, and change of employment are just a few examples. The economic challenges vary according to whether the mothers and fathers are never married, divorced, separated, or widowed. Poverty and economic insecurities of single parents are the result of the low earnings capacity of single mothers, the lack of child support from the ex-spouse, and the meager benefits accorded by public assistance programs. The startling fact is clear: one out of two mother-only families are poor, and in these families poverty lasts much longer.

Women face an uphill battle in digging out of poverty caused by divorce. The have low income, must provide child support, and may have little work experience, which puts them in a lower economic group. It is an illusion that fathers pay child support. At best only 40 percent of fathers pay child support of any kind. In most cases they do not pay all they owe. Their meager allowance will not even pay for childcare.

Social Concerns of Single Parents

Single parents not only face economic concerns including unemployment, but their children also face social development problems such as dropping out of school and forming mother-only families themselves. In a mother-only family mom becomes the daddy, too. Unfortunately being a single parent may lower a mother's self-esteem. Being a single parent because of a broken marriage makes one feel rejected and dejected. Single moms often experience role over-load because they assume both father and mother roles and do not feel adequate as a parent because of household tasks, childcare, and economic pressures.

Church Ministry with Single Parents

Churches can minister to single parents by remembering that single-parent families have three needs: redemption/rehabilitation, acceptance and love, and to belong or not be lonely. Here's a brief list of ministries some churches provide for single parents:

- Holiday events
- Big brothers and big sisters to provide counseling experiences and role modeling

• Emotional support and practical advice to assist single parents in coping with their many demands

Some churches have single parents participating in ministry by:

• Offering family life education programs especially for single parents

• Including them in leadership positions in Sunday School and other activities

• Providing awareness of community resources such as health services, family counseling services, and job training opportunities

• Sponsoring single parents conferences, support groups, and Sunday School classes

• Having the pastor lead discussions of special concerns to groups of single parents

If you are reading this article and are a single parent yourself, consider building a support system. Support systems, people on whom we can depend particularly during times of stress, are important to all parents. Single parents might try the following tips for building a support system:

• Identify people you are convinced you can rely on.

• Write beside each name what that person can offer you (sympathy, motivation, guidance, planning, recreation, etc.).

• Place a checkmark by what you need right now. Number your needs in order of importance.

• Write out how you can ask the right support person for what you want.

• Plan a time to call or see your priority people.

Single Fathers Are Parents, Too

For the most part, fathers have been ignored when consideration is given to the adjustments of divorced parents and their children. Most information has dealt with the parent in custody, and in most cases this parent is the mother. It is not surprising, however, to find that fathers do care and are anxious about proper adjustments.

Even though a father may visit his children on a regular basis, circumstances are often strained. Such terms as "weekend father," and "Uncle Dad" indicate that the father is supplemental and not really necessary for his children anymore. When they go to movies on Saturday with their children, they can spot other single dads sitting alongside their children. Single dads blame themselves for their children's shortcomings. They carry around feelings of guilt, anger, confusion, reconciliation, and healing.

The single dad faces the feeling of being disqualified from speaking out, even in serious crisis moments. He feels parental pain because he cannot see his children every day and play a vital role in their lives. So some single dads overcompensate for their failures by becoming entertainers and gift givers, as they try to buy a bit of affection and respect while also trying to deal with the guilt over the divorce.

The children catch on. Daddy can buy me what I need and want. Mom is too strapped financially because of dad's lack of child support. If handled poorly by both parents, the father's visitation rights could become the saddest aspects of the divorce. These visits begin in anxiety and end in boredom.

The key is not how much time is spent with the children but rather the quality of that time. Single dads should not feel that they have to spend the rest of their lives dating their children. Admittedly, when they are with their children, they may feel that they need to be "double-time" parents. More than gifts and movies children need fathers to relax with them and be involved with their lives.

AdultApplication: How can finances be a problem for the single parent? Why is the loss of identity a problem for single parents? Why do single parents have problems with self-esteem? What are the major problems associated with child rearing that face the single parent? How is the loss of intimacy a problem for single parents? How is disruption a problem for the single parent?

_____

_____

Work! Work! Work!

How do you think about working? Is it mere drudgery? Is it a means to an end—income? We spend approximately one-third of our life working. Why do we grow up beyond the youth years? To work, of course! To be a grownup is to be ready to work. To be "grown up" is to be busy—at work. This article outlines ways contemporary adults examine their work lives and apply Christian values to this significant part of their daily living.

Before World War II, female employment was largely restricted to the unmarried. After marriage or the birth of a child, most women withdrew from the workplace. After the War, in the early 50s there were far fewer unmarried women to fill those employment vacancies. At that time jobs were more tightly gender stratified, and employers had no alternative but to begin hiring married women to fill jobs previously filled by unmarried women. Added to that was the rise in the continuing education movement in the 60s, which allowed married women to move into new employment.

These changes have resulted in a resetting of the social clock. So the woman returning to the work force is younger because she has been absent from the labor force for a shorter period of time. Today and for the past 20 years, more and more women are either returning to the work force or have never left it, despite establishing families and becoming mothers.

The earlier dictum, of "one job for life" no longer holds. The odds of a person's staying in one job for life are getting slimmer all the time. These developments mean that we can now think of work as we do our lives—in terms of the seasons of life. Work and vocation have different meanings as we age. Young adults should no longer count on a linear experience of education in their 20s, working until 65, and then retiring. More and more young adults are adapting to a parallel life course of working, breaking away from work for further skill development or additional schooling, then returning to the same or a different job.

Adults in their middle years have a different perspective on working. They face new challenges such as shrinking opportunities for promotion and pressure from the younger generation. Plus, they face the unwillingness of the older generation to retire, which further limits their career opportunities. Older boomers face the possibilities of work life in their 50s as a dull, boring trap. Accordingly, they should rethink their leisure commitments and start thinking about part-time work, hobbies, or other ways of maintaining identifiable and satisfying interests.

Church leaders with adults should focus on the meaning of work to their daily lives. Many workers face burnout, an employee's loss of enthusiasm for doing their jobs. This trauma is especially seen with those in helping professions such as medicine, teaching, and social work. Another problem is alienation, which occurs when workers feel their work is unimportant and uninteresting. No doubt you have seen alienation in large factories in which a worker is not recognized as a person but merely as a drone who performs a repetitive task. In a positive turn, middle-age adults often redefine their work goals and invest less of their ego in their job and take a more relaxed approach to their work.

How should believers evaluate their work according to God's standards? The Bible gives ample evidence of reasons to work:

- To fulfill God's plan—Genesis 2:15; Psalms 104:19-24; Isaiah 28:23-29
- To earn a living—2 Thessalonians 3:10
- To avoid idleness—1 Thessalonians 4:11; 1 Timothy 5:13
- To share with others—Ephesians 4:28
- To be a testimony—1 Timothy 6:1-2
- To honor God—Ephesians 6:6-8

Christians should obey the injunctions of Scripture, rather than their feelings, when deciding about their attitudes toward work. Genesis 2:15 offers a positive outlook on work. Adam is expected to till and keep the field in the garden. Thus work, even in paradise, is part of human fulfillment. God does not intend us to partake in mindless labor just to keep us busy. Instead, in this instance God has entrusted the field to Adam; he is in charge of the work to be done. Of course in the Fall, man realizes obstacles to satisfaction and joy in one's work. Even with that, work is not considered a punishment. Everything, and everyone, created by God, is good. Work is good because God created it. What has changed is that we now see that our work builds up the kingdom and we are cocreators with God. Work can give meaning to our existence, open up channels for our creativity, and offer us means to help others. The way back to the paradise model of work is to collaborate with God, and this means adopting His standards for work, not our own.

The Bible does not describe a detailed plan for owners and workers. What we know about cooperation, equality, and harmony in the workplace we learn from Bible teachings on unity, oneness, and the common good. For instance, Philippians 2:4 says, "Each of you should look not only to your own interests, but also to the interests of others." Christian managers, foremen, and others employers should obey this biblical injunction toward their employees. Furthermore, women earn significantly less than men earn. In America the ratio of female to male earning is about 0.75, a figure that is typical of other developing countries. Disabled women, for instance, are paid less than disabled men are paid. The Bible clearly brings good news to today's women: "There is neither Jew nor Greek, slave nor free, male nor female, for you are all one in Christ Jesus" (Gal. 3:28).

AdultApplication: Can a person be under the judgment of God because of his work? How should a Christian choose an occupation? What are some considerations for meaningful and fulfilling employment? What are some dangers inherent in our work? How may one give a Christian witness at work?

Do you know how members of your class or in your church feel about their work? How can your class share the excitement of a young professional on the way up? help someone who has lost a job? encourage those who are losing their enthusiasm for their work, feel trapped in a dead-end job, or are holding on for retirement?

_____

_____

The Real Senior Adult

Nobody grows old by living
   A number of years.
People grow old from lack of purpose.
   Years wrinkle the skin.
Lack of purpose wrinkles the soul.
> —Author unknown

Harlan Sanders, founder of the Kentucky Fried Chicken Corporation, gave some excellent advice to guide in our study of the senior adult years:

> There is these days a whole lot of talk and a whole lot of writing about why adults act certain ways at certain ages. We are told that when we are 35 years old we act one way and that 10 years later we act differently. All of this is just fine; discovering these things is what research is all about. But I hope that our young people who have their careers ahead of them will keep one thing in mind. It's a pretty simple thing, too. Let's not hang a tag on folks at a certain age and pretend that everyone wearing that tag is just like everyone else with the same tag (Harlan Sanders, 1977, "Education and the Preparation for Retirement," *Educational Gerontology: An International Journal,* 1993, 3).

Such an attitude of discrimination toward seniors is a form of prejudice, namely ageism. Seniors in our society face prejudice just because they are growing old. They are devalued—seen as losers and not winners as the young are.

Why this devaluation of the aged? Myths and stereotypes hinder our perception and understanding of older persons. Consider these false perceptions:

- Senility inevitably accompanies old age.
- Most old people are isolated from their families.
- The majority of old people are in poor health.
- Older people are more likely than younger people to be crime victims.
- The majority of older people live in poverty.
- Older people tend to become more religious as they age.

Understanding Today's Adults: 25 Years and Older

• Older workers are less productive than younger ones.

• Old people who retire usually suffer a decline in health and an early death.

• Most old people have no interest in, or capacity for, sexual relations.

• Most old people end up in nursing homes and other long-term care institutions.

Many adults are driven by new circumstances caused by demographic changes and healthcare advances. As the fabled baby boomers begin to hit 65 in 2010, they will remake our ideas of growing old. Their values will be decidedly different from the oldest-old cohort of today. Hopefully we will see that growing old is a version of growing up, not an accident, but normal.

<u>AdultApplication:</u> Talk with some senior adults in your church about these stereotypes. Ask them for their impressions. Compare their responses with the following quiz.

How do you look at the senior years? Take this test.

This quiz takes less than 10 minutes to complete. Remember when responding to the questions that this quiz does not focus on any specific age range of adults; instead it focuses on adults as they age. Circle "T" for true or "F" for false to indicate your opinion about each statement.

T / F   1. Vision tends to decline with age.

T / F   2. Hearing tends to decrease with age.

T / F   3. Ability to adapt to external temperature changes tends to decline with age.

T / F   4. Time required to react to a stimulus tends to rise with age.

T / F   5. Anxiety tends to decrease with age.

T / F   6. Cautiousness tends to rise with age.

T / F   7. Performance after reprimand tends to rise with age.

T / F   8. Risk-taking tends to increase with age.

T / F   9. Self-concept tends to rise and then decline with age.

T / F 10. Pace of learning tends to decline with age.

T / F 11. The need to relate new information to current knowledge tends to decrease with age.

T / F 12. Ability to learn complex material tends to increase with age.

T / F 13. Abstract reasoning tends to rise with age.

T / F 14. Short-term memory tends to rise with age.

T / F 15. Accumulation of knowledge tends to decline with age.

T / F 16. The learning process tends to change with age.

T / F 17. Ability to learn tends to remain stable with age.

T / F 18. Data collection for decision-making tends to decrease with age.

T / F 19. Information overload tends to decline with age.

T / F 20. Time required to make a decision tends to increase with age.

T / F 21. Conservativeness in decision-making tends to increase with age.

T / F 22. Review of previously successful solutions for problem solving tends to increase with age.

T / F 23. Importance of experience in decision-making tends to decline with age.

T / F 24. Accuracy of work tends to decrease with age.

T / F 25. Rate of worker output tends to decrease with age.

T / F 26. Consistency of worker output tends to decline with age.

T / F 27. Timed performance tends to decline with age.

T / F 28. Untimed performance tends to remain stable with age.

T / F 29. Individual differences in performance tend to decrease with age.

T / F 30. Job turnover tends to decrease with age.

T / F 31. Worker absenteeism tends to rise with age.

T / F 32. Worker satisfaction tends to remain stable with age.

T / F 33. Work performance tends to remain stable with age.

T / F 34. Chronic health conditions tend to decline with age.

T / F 35. Short-term health conditions tend to increase with age.

T / F 36. Recovery time from health conditions and injuries tends to rise with age.

T / F 37. Severity of work injury tends to decrease with age.

T / F 38. Frequency of work injury tends to rise with age.

T / F 39. Risk of work injury tends to decrease with age.

T / F 40. Total costs of work injury tend to decline with age.

Now compare your answers with the correct ones.

Items 1–4 (Biology)   Items 5–9 (Psychology)

Items 10–17 (Learning)   Items 18–23 (Decision-making)

Items 24–33 (Work Performance)   Items 34–40 (Health)

(Answers: 1 T, 2 T, 3 T, 4 T, 5 F, 6 T, 7 F, 8 F, 9 T, 10 T, 11 F, 12 F, 13 F, 14 F, 15 F, 16 T, 17 T, 18 F, 19 F, 20 T, 21 F, 22 T, 23 F, 24 F, 25 T, 26 F, 27 T, 28 T, 29 F, 30 T, 31 F, 32 T, 33 T, 34 F, 35 F, 36 T, 37 F, 38 F, 39 T, 40 T)

Test used by permission from Michael Galbreth, Florida Atlantic University at Boca Raton.

AdultApplication: Which answers were the most surprising for you? Why? What do the results of this study say to church ministry with aging adults? What stereotypes of aging persons does this quiz reveal? What positive aspects of aging does this quiz reveal? What do the results of this quiz suggest about your church's ministry with elders?

Understanding Today's Adults: 25 Years and Older

On Friday, January 16, 1998, NASA announced a return to orbit for John Glenn, the first American to orbit the Earth. He asked NASA if he could fly again to conduct space-based research on aging. Thirty-six years earlier, on February 20, 1962, Glenn climbed into his Friendship 7 Mercury capsule and lifted off on an Atlas 6 rocket. His orbital flight lasted 4 hours, 55 minutes, all but 7 minutes being in weightlessness. Glenn became the first American to orbit the Earth and an instant hero. The 77-year-old senator from Ohio showed that young people would look at older persons with new appreciation. With his exceptional flight he shattered many myths of aging. He showed that seniors need a vision and a dream for their later years.

Our concepts of aging reflect a lifetime of attitudes, biases, and experiences.

• Most seniors have positive views of their aging.

• Aging is universal; everyone is aging at the same rate.

• Aging is normal; it is not an accident or a cruel trick from the Almighty.

• Aging is inevitable.

• It is variable; not all people age in the same way. For instance, regular physical exercise, proper diet, regular checkups, and not smoking will pay great dividends as we grow older.

In response, seniors can and do learn anything they choose to learn. They can and do change. In fact, they live in a world of change. More importantly, elders want to be self-directed and are vital human beings.

AdultApplication: How do you look at your own aging? How do you look at older people in your church?

_____

_____

_____

_____

Over time society's attitudes toward the elderly have been shaped into several theories. We will look at two approaches and how they may shape attitudes toward the elderly in our churches.

Disengagement—According to this approach, disengagement by elders is a gradual but inevitable withdrawal from the various roles and responsibilities of middle adulthood. Both society and the elderly withdraw from each other. In churches, elders "retire" from church leadership positions just as they retire from school teaching or working on the assembly line. They say, "I've done all I can do; let some young people take over."

From society's perspective this theory means younger people can't depend on elders any longer because they are not producing anything; and anyway, they are going to die. They are at the dying stage of life, not the living.

This approach is played out in the expression of the 23-year-old aspiring church leader who said, "When I get to that church, the first thing I will do is take out the organ!" The "old," represented by the organ, was deemed to be worthless now that the new was on the scene—represented by him.

This approach also has another dangerous dimension. It becomes prescriptive, not just descriptive. That is, elders will begin to sense that disengaging from life is what they should do; it is their duty toward society and to the church.

AdultApplication: Do you know of any attitudes or activities in your church that represent the disengagement approach to aging?

_____

_____

_____

Activity approach to aging—The activity approach was developed in response to the disengagement approach. The activity approach suggests that we withdraw from some activities in middle age and substitute new activities as we age. So a middle manager of an auto parts firm retires and volunteers with the Retired Service Volunteer Program. Or a landscape architect retires and volunteers to plan and develop a garden near the children's playground at the church.

The thinking goes that persons substitute appropriate social, physical, and mental activities for those they had in middle adulthood. This seems to be the dominant approach behind many government programs, especially at senior centers. It, too, has some shortcomings. For instance, can't a person merely rest during retirement and not clog up their week with activity after activity? For another thing, Christians need to see beyond a person's output or activity and value the person whether or not the person is busy. Being is far more important than doing.

Society has the unfortunate idea that we need to have lots of activities for older church members to "keep granny off the street." I believe this thinking about the preferred patterns of aging got its root in youth activity programming, which was prominent in many areas in the 60s—that is, keep youth, now seniors, busy, busy, busy.

This approach implies that social activity is the essence of life, and we must be active to achieve life satisfaction. Think about the number of persons in long-term care who cannot be active, though they wish they could be. They are hampered by Parkinson's Disease or arthritis and cannot be active. Furthermore, this separation between the active and those unable to be active drives an unnecessary wedge between persons. It can be prejudicial. Society brands elders into two groups: the haves who can be active, and the have-nots who cannot be active.

AdultApplication: Do you know of any attitudes or activities in your church that represent the activity approach to aging?

_____

_____

Retirement

We may need to rethink our traditional views about retirement. Already older baby boomers are reshaping how we think about the life span. We now considers life to be divided into thirds: the first 30 years in education, the second 30 years in vocation, and the final 30 years in "retirement." On the downside of this is a peculiar dilemma. If we don't extend the minimum age for retirement, we may find many people running out of money before they run out of life. But extending the retirement age puts strains on young adults who are waiting for entry-level jobs to open up.

The year 1996 was a watershed as the leading edge of the baby boomers turned 50. It comes as no surprise that our nation is becoming older. As a result, parties to celebrate the Big 5-0 in the last decade will continue in the early decades of the 21st century as those same persons celebrate their Big 6-0 and Big 7-0. In fact, as one wag has said, "You better enjoy golf while you can, because all the tee times will be taken beginning in 2010!" (when the leading edge of the boomers hits 65). And with the average age of retirement moving steadily downward, it may be sooner than we realize.

For further reading:

- *Forward Together: A New Vision for Senior Adult Ministry*
  by Jay Johnston (Nashville: LifeWay Church Resources)
- *Golden Opportunities: Ministry Ideas for Senior Adults*
  by Nancy Elliott (Birmingham: New Hope Press)
- *Senior Adult Choir Ministry: Age Is No Excuse*
  by Lyndell Vaught (Nashville: LifeWay Church Resources)

AdultApplication: How many adults in your church are currently retired? How will this change in the next few decades? How is your church preparing for this change? How is your church helping adults prepare for their own retirement? (for example, seminars on financial planning, training for part-time employment or volunteer work, planning for activities and ministries to engage senior adults).

Major Concerns of the Elderly

What are the major concerns of the elderly? One research report indicated that the two major issues are declining health and lack of money, followed by anticipated loss of mental health faculties, being dependent on others, and becoming dependent on family. The elderly worry least about being isolated or alone and living in a nursing facility (AARP, 1999). As with other age groups, seniors researchers have classified older persons into various strata in order to understand them. Herb Shore, veteran gerontologist, has developed an overview of the aging adult (see the chart on p. 51).

Another age range for seniors posits three generations. The "young old" are 65–74. "Middle old" seniors are 75–85, and the "old old" are 85 plus. As you might imagine, age is not always a reliable indication of an elder's quality of life. Another description of the senior years helps church leaders to understand their needs:

Continuity with middle age—This period is characterized by continuing many of the activities of middle age without the burden of employment. Some carry over skills learned in employment into retirement, as a teacher who now volunteers to tutor children.

- Retirement plans pursued
- Middle-age lifestyle continued
- Other activities substituted for work

Early transition—The most common events for this period were the onset of ill health, the death of a spouse, or the need to move. A widow said that her new station in life was like being sawed in two: one half is thrown away; the other is told to "get over it." An older man was deprived of reading and driving when he had a stroke.

- Involuntary transitional events
- Voluntary transitional events

Revised lifestyle—Seniors feel the need for affiliation with others who share their lifestyle during this period. They want the company of other people. This may mean revised life objectives, including finding ways to deal with loneliness.

• Adaptation to changes of early transition

• Stable lifestyle appropriate to older adulthood

• Socialization realized through age-group affiliation

Later transition—In this period elders begin to experience loss in several areas.

• Loss of health and mobility

• Need for assistance and/or care

• Loss of autonomy

Final period

• Adaptation to changes of later transition

• Stable lifestyle appropriate to level of dependency

• Sense of finitude, mortality

(James Fisher, "A Framework for Describing Developmental Change Among Adults," *Adult Education Quarterly,* 1993.)

Fisher's framework may prove helpful to church leaders charged with planning educational programs and activities for older persons. Each stage has both potential and challenges for the elderly. Fisher's framework also has application to grouping and grading adults in Sunday School. Few churches have a strict age-grading system through the adult years, that is, all persons 79–84 belong in one class. Instead of strict age grading for seniors, consider a class or department for each period. This allows seniors to be grouped not by strict age grading but by lifestyle. One caution: grouping all persons in the final period will mean the development of specialized homebound departments when these persons cannot attend church on a regular basis.

AdultApplication: Interview some elders in your church or family. Ask them to rate themselves on a scale of 1 to 5 according to Fisher's framework. To what extent do these phase descriptions apply to them? You may want to extend the discussion by asking them how their Christian faith affects and strengthens them during their later maturity.

AN OVERVIEW OF THE AGING ADULT

Group	% of Older Adults	Health Status	Money Status	Activity Status	Support	Living
GO-GO 65–74 Independent Invisible	15%	Well Physically & Mentally	Adequate	Adequate to Frisky	Great	Full
GO SLOW 65–74 Interdependent Not always seen	35%	Well Physically & Mentally	Adequate	Adequate	Adequate	Increased Dependence
SLOW GO 74–84 Semi-dependent	25%	Well Physically & Mentally	Mediocre	Mediocre	Risky	More dependent
CAN'T GO 74–84 Slow slow Dependent prone	10%	Ill Physically & Mentally	Declining	Declining	Walking Wounded	Needs Assistance
NO GO 85+ Dependent Impaired Poor, sick "Old old"	15%	Ill Physically & Mentally	Declining	Declining	Frail, At Risk	Institutionalized or More Restricted

Herb Shore, Association of Jewish Homes for Aging, Dallas, Texas

Understanding Today's Adults: 25 Years and Older

Caregiving

In recent years the term caregiving has broadened from a term describing the care of children and infants to include care for the elderly, primarily by women. In fact, this is a second career for some middle-age adults. The following chart parallels the kinds of feelings, situations, and responses of the caregiver and the older family member, as well as ways to solve issues between them.

Caregiver's Feelings	*Older Family Member's Feelings*
Love	Love
Concern	Loneliness
Anxiety	Depression (losses)
Stress	Fear (changes)
Fatigue	Illness
Depression	Dependence
Frustration	Helplessness
Exploitation	Physical complaints
Guilt	Manipulative behavior
Resentment	Paranoid behavior
Anger	Hostility
Hostility	Anger
Helplessness	Fear of own aging

Adults who are providing care for aging parents need ministry. The following suggestions are useful in ministering to these families.
- Assist family members in understanding the physical and psychological aging process.
- Provide education opportunities for caregivers about legal issues, financial issues, living wills, emotional needs and responses, etc.
- Assist caregivers and older family members in enhancing communication among family members.
- Assist caregivers in the use of internal and external support systems.

- Assist caregivers in finding and using community resources.
- Provide counseling services, including support groups with the purpose of decreasing family problems and conflicts.

Poll your friends over 50. Because of better health care and improved medical care, many of them are dealing with aging parents. Adults are surviving to the age of decline. And because of radically changed social patterns, the once familiar choice of inviting mother to move in is less automatic and far less feasible. When these two generations attempt to join together, it's like joining two different time zones: elders are from Greenwich, and older boomers are from Pacific Standard Time.

"I'm a caregiver." The term doesn't ring with familiarity. We recognize the term and predictable routine behind the statement, "I'm a mother." The latter has status. The former implies a lower, accidental position. Caregiving is not highly valued in Western society. It does not create evidence that the effort has value when weighed against salary and prestige. In this century caregiving is changing precisely because there are more elderly who are living longer and because the number of potential caregivers is decreasing. This is caused in part because families are smaller than in an earlier era and because daughters, the usual caregivers, are involved in careers. Caregiving is generally and usually provided for those who are considered "ill," whereas mothering (another caregiving role) is usually with well persons. Who are the persons to whom caregivers extend concern? These are persons who are:

- Experiencing an acute illness
- Experiencing a chronic illness
- In pain
- Recovering from an acute illness or health accident—
  for example, a stroke
- Experiencing long-term disabilities

Who cares for these people in our contemporary society? Caregiving is a more pressing issue today for a number of reasons. First, more seniors need care. Second, the usual caregiver is a woman, and those women face a crisis of deciding how they will manage career and caregiving responsibilities at the same time. Generally women care for the elderly; men give money. Consequently, women face special challenges.

• Many women have to face the choice of caring for an aging parent or continuing their careers.

• Families are smaller, consequently fewer children can assist with caregiving responsibilities

• More and more women are single parents. They need assistance with caring for two generations simultaneously.

One family member usually becomes the primary caregiver and bears the brunt of caregiving responsibilities, while others occupy secondary roles for three reasons: choice, designation, or default. Why this design? Cultural values, even more than financial considerations, appear to be a major contributing factor when the decision is made to take care of mother. In working-class families the parents are the ones who often choose which of their children will become identified as the primary caregiver.

Despite these arrangements adults resist this designation. Caregivers in their 30s say, "I'm too young for this to be happening to me." Caregivers in middle age say, "I thought I'd be free at this time of my life. I wanted to enjoy retirement, maybe do a little traveling; my empty nest is being refilled." Older caregivers say, "I'm too old for this. I'm old myself." In fact, the number of grandchildren who are helping with two generations is on the rise. It is expected that this rate will increase given the population growth among the very old.

The caregiving task faced by many adults is intensively demanding. Caring for aging parents can be a joy, however, an opportunity to give back across the generations. Church leaders should be sensitive to the anguish of middle adults who are daily watching their parents deteriorate by the ravages of Alzheimer's disease or face lonely days in a nursing facility eight hundred miles away.

For further reading:

• *Forward Together: A New Vision for Senior Adult Ministry* by Jay Johnston (Nashville: LifeWay Church Resources)

• *Ideas for Homebound Ministries* by Malcolm Masler (Birmingham: Woman's Missionary Union)

AdultApplication: Every church has adults who are caring for aging parents. How can your church provide care for the caregiver? What can churches do to help middle adults with their aging parents? Interview some adults in this situation and ask them about their needs. They may have questions about processes for which others in the church can provide answers based on experience or knowledge—for example, getting power of attorney, transitioning all financial responsibilities from parent to child, finding a good long-term care facility, etc. Or they may just need encouragement or support. What can your church do to help?

_____

_____

_____

_____

_____

_____

_____

Ways Adults Learn

How do adults learn faith? For some, true faith cannot be learned; it is only absorbed through worship, meditation on the Bible, and attending conferences.

Several years ago I was teaching a coed class for couples in their 30s. After class I casually asked a woman why she attended Adult Sunday School. Her response was disappointing yet not surprising. Her answer was, "I'm here because of my children." She attended regularly and contributed generously to the lesson discussion. But her frank admission of her motivation indicated that she was just "doing time" in my classroom while her children were engaged in Bible study.

What was she saying? She indicated that she already knew all the stories. She was familiar with key Bible passages. She knew all the Sunday School answers. She had no need for any further spiritual growth because she, at age 34, had arrived and needed no more Christian growth. Her children needed to learn in Sunday School, but she did not.

I learned from that experience: she did not need more and more information about Scripture that she had learned from her own childhood. I did not need to study harder to bring out things that she might not remember. How could I challenge her to engage in adult discipleship? I realized that merely wanting my class to attend more regularly was a low and superficial description.

One of the hallmarks of Christian living to which adults are particularly suited is Christian living as vocation. I am not suggesting that all adults need to become professional ministers—not in the least. We move through life not just with our feet or by the calendar as one day replaces another. But we are moved by the compelling call of God. Life depends on us, even as we depend on God. Not only do we have a calling, but we also live in dependence upon God our Maker. Frederick Buechner, in *Wishful Thinking, a Theological ABC* (Harper & Row, 1973), provides a lively description of this double dependence.

It comes from the Latin *vocare,* to call, and means the work one is called to by God. There are all different kinds of voices calling you to all different kinds of work, and the problem is to find out which is the voice of God rather than of Society, say, or the Superego, or Self-Interest.

By and large, a good rule for finding out is this: The kind of work God usually calls you to is the kind of work (a) that you need most to do and (b) that the world most needs to have done. If you really get a kick out of your work, you've presumably met requirement (a), but if your work is writing TV deodorant commercials, the chances are you've missed requirement (b). On the other hand, if your work is being a doctor in a leper colony, you have probably met requirement (b), but if most of the time you're bored and depressed by it, the chances are you have not only bypassed (a) but probably aren't helping your patients much either. The place God calls you to is the place where your deep gladness and the world's deep hunger meet.

The second metaphor, which describes adult discipleship, is *journey*. Paul said, "Forgetting what is behind and straining toward what is ahead, I press on toward the goal to win the prize for which God has called me heavenward in Christ Jesus" (Phil. 3:13-14).

Spiritual reflection is one avenue for this journey. Thousands have practiced it as they worked through various books such as *Experiencing God*. Spiritual reflection may be an outgrowth of one's daily Bible study and prayer. It may concur with moments of despair or joy. Usually spiritual reflection happens when assessing one's life story or a portion of it. While it is easy to assess and contemplate the mere facts of one's life, especially in adulthood, one may also attach meaning to those events. So life is understood by tracing the finger of God through various life experiences.

How can an adult incorporate spiritual reflection into the disciplines of life? The method is to ask reflective questions about how God is, or can be, involved in life activities. Persons interpret the past by asking, "What did God teach me about myself? about others? about His created order?"

In the present tense adults can examine and imagine how God could be working with us and through us in the future. We can ask questions such as: "How is God related to my life today? Is this what God expects of me? Is this God's will for my life? Would this advance the kingdom of God? How would the rich resources of the Christian faith help me?"

Spiritual reflection consists of laying our stories alongside the biblical story to give us guidance in daily living. Though talking about pastoral theology, C. W. Brister's comments in *Pastoral Care in the Church* (HarperCollins, 1992) apply to spiritual reflection as well. "Pastoral theology at its best interfaces the oughtness of the Scriptures with the isness of existence, so that human experience is brought to fullest self-awareness and accountability in intimate engagement with divine Reality." So the cycle moves from action or life events to reflection, to action. Through theological or spiritual reflection believers think about their life in biblical context.

Scripture tells us that we ought to love God with our heart, our emotions—and many believers feel that this is the only legitimate way to relate to God. However, on the same page is the admonition to love God with all our minds. Adult believers can love God with their minds when they make sure that their beliefs are in accordance with an orderly formulation of biblical truth. Because Christians have different understandings of God, the mission of the church, the Holy Spirit, and the person and work of Christ, it is inevitable that differences of opinion erupt in the adult years. Some would offer a minimum requirement—we must only agree on the minimum doctrine. Others go to the other extreme and attempt to force everyone to agree with every one of their theological presuppositions. Whether in the home during private reflections, or in the midst of sermon or song, or in small-group Bible studies, adults are engaged in theological reflection. It is often hard work, but it is also spiritually rewarding, resulting in greater discipleship.

"The church's theological essence sets her apart from other social organizations such as a welfare agency, a psychotherapy clinic, a social club, or an aesthetic experience. A fundamental purpose of theology is to guide and serve the process of church formation, preservation, and mission—that is, to enable the church to realize her essence to be a community of faith, hope, and love"

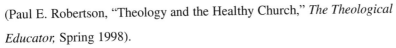
(Paul E. Robertson, "Theology and the Healthy Church," *The Theological Educator,* Spring 1998).

For teaching suggestions, use the resource *Teaching Adults: A Guide for Transformational Teaching* by Rick Edwards (Nashville: LifeWay Church Resources).

For curriculum resources, consider the following:

Sunday School (available by calling 1–800–458–2772)

Explore the Bible

Family Bible Study for Adults

Discipleship Training (available by calling 1–800–458–2772)

Baptist Adults

Adults on Mission (available by calling 1–800–968–7301)

Dimensions

Missons Mosaic

Women on Mission (available by calling 1–800–968–7301)

Missions Mosaic

Baptist Men on Mission (available by calling 1–800–448–8032)

Missions in Motion

AdultApplication: Do you think the better image of growing adult discipleship is vocation or journey? What examples from your own life or the lives of your class members support your answer? Are adults in your church encouraged in personal worship/daily prayer and Bible study? How can you plan times for personal reflection for adults to consider their own growth and encourage others to grow spiritually?

_____

_____

_____

Teaching Adults Who Have Learning Disabilities

Kevin is 25 years old. At 7, he was diagnosed with a verbal learning disability that affected his reading and oral expression. He struggled through school but managed to graduate from high school with help from his family, tutors, teachers, and friends.

Kevin was involved in church until he reached his junior year in high school. He recalls the day he decided he no longer wanted to go to church. His Sunday School teacher required the class to memorize a set of Bible verses she said would help them as they approached their college years. Kevin took the assignment seriously, and for him it was a disaster. He struggled to read and comprehend the Bible verses. And although he was able to read them, he was unable to memorize them. He rarely could memorize vocabulary words for Spanish, much less whole Bible verses. Kevin told his mother that he would never return to this class. Gradually he dropped out of church altogether.

How Common Are Learning Disabilities?

According to information from the National Institutes of Health, 15–20 percent of the U.S. population have some form of learning disability. Most individuals who manifest learning disabilities have deficits in reading or in the processing of language (e.g., understanding what is said or in succinctly organizing a response). Most experts agree that more boys than girls (some researchers suggest approximately a 3:2 ratio) are likely to have learning disabilities.

What Is a Learning Disability and How Does a Disability Develop?

Controversies continue about a clear definition and criteria to be used to diagnose a learning disability; however, most experts agree there are different types of learning disabilities. Subtypes of learning disabilities include: (1) dyslexia (a verbal learning disability that impairs reading, spelling, verbal memory tasks, and rapid naming); (2) dyscalculia (a disability that impairs math skills due to spatial organizational problems, sequencing difficulties, poor graphomotor control, inadequate attention to visual detail, and poor number logic); (3) dysgraphia (a writing disability; however, there are limited studies in this area).

Adults with a diagnosis of dyslexia make up the largest group. A smaller number of individuals have deficits in visual-spatial cognition (nonverbal learning disabilities) and experience significant difficulty conceptually understanding math or have poor handwriting and appear to be motor clumsy. In addition, over the last 15–20 years, concern has grown for individuals who experience significant difficulty in social situations. These individuals experience difficulty interpreting the behavior of others, such as gestures and facial expressions; thus, they may appear to be socially awkward and experience limited skills interacting with others.

Adults who have learning disabilities are likely to experience poor reading comprehension, slow reading rate, laborious writing, slow processing of new information, poor mathematical skills, and/or secondary emotional or behavioral problems, such as depression, poor self-esteem, somatic complaints, anxiety disorders, and social problems.

While the causes of learning disabilities remain unknown, a genetic basis is likely. Risk factors cited in research literature associated with learning disabilities include: (1) the presence of learning disabilities in other family members; (2) a very low birth rate; (3) head traumas; (4) seizure disorders; and (5) radiation therapy treatment for long-term survivors of acute lymphocytic leukemia.

Many laypeople mistakenly associate low intelligence or laziness with a learning disability. While each person with a learning disability is unique, one of the most common factors noted in these individuals is that they tend to achieve significantly below their intellectual abilities even though they are of average or above average intelligence.

What Is the Prognosis for Individuals with Learning Disabilities?

"I can read pretty good now, but it takes me much longer than it does my wife. My spelling is terrible, too."

Despite their disabilities, many people achieve functional reading skills. They can read the newspaper and most material at work. Most continue, however, to read at levels that do not match their intellectual abilities. Most adults with learning disabilities report that they rarely read for pleasure, even though they remain curious and possess a desire to learn. They just adopt other methods to acquire information. They may do this by carefully listening and watching educational or news programs on television.

A learning disability is a chronic problem that does not go away with maturity. Research has suggested that even if an individual with a learning disability graduates from college, he or she is at high risk for job dissatisfaction. Thus diminished feelings of self-worth continue to plague many adults with learning disabilities.

However, an important positive influence in the lives of adults with learning disabilities is a strong family support system. The church can serve as an extended support system, and this support system is significant even when the person with a learning disability has a strong family support system. If you teach a person with a learning disability, you may be a vital link for acceptance between a person with learning disabilities and his or her peers.

What Can I Do to Help an Individual with a Learning Disability?

First, increase your efforts to empower and encourage the individual with a learning disability. You can do this by helping that person feel safe in the class and church environment. Don't set up the individual for embarrassment or failure by asking him or her to read a passage of the Bible aloud before he has read it silently.

Deborah Hancock's article in the Winter 1998–99 issue of Life and Work: *Directions* entitled, "He Can Hardly Read and He's in My Class," offers examples of approaches that can result in embarrassment and/or alienation for the individual with a reading problem. The person with a learning disability is more than able to participate in your Sunday School class if you create an atmosphere in which everyone makes an effort to accept all individuals and it is tailored to fit the unique needs of its participants. Every class member is responsible for creating an emotionally safe environment.

Evidence now supports the use of strategy and organizational instruction for individuals with learning disabilities rather than an approach that uses the lecture and a "take-a-turn" approach to reading the Bible. Strategy instruction provides a framework for thinking as well as techniques for teaching concepts and truths. This approach works well for an individual with any kind of language-related learning disabilities (i.e., problems with reading, understanding language, or expressing himself/herself) or for the individual with memory problems. This approach can be helpful for all participants in your class.

Here are some steps to using strategy instruction in your adult groups:

1. Prior to launching into the details of the discussion, provide a clear idea of the central concept (or "big idea") for the lesson. One possible approach to share this with the class is by preparing a handout of this statement with several letters deleted in key words. For example, "Jesus offers God's f ___ ___ g ___ ___ ___ n ___ ___ ___ and restoration, not condemnation, to those who have broken God's l ___ ___ ___."

By distributing this at the beginning of the lesson, the individual with learning disabilities will be able to listen more attentively and effectively. Discuss the meanings of more difficult words or modify the language. For example, the big idea mentioned could be restated: "Jesus offers God's forgiveness, not blame, to those who have broken God's laws." Discuss what this means in everyday language.

2. If the discussion has a number of concepts that seem important, sift through the possible concepts and determine the most important ones. A well-organized and well-supported lesson can be retained more easily than one that focuses on the details in the passages in a hit-and-miss approach. Provide the class with a written outline of the discussion with the main ideas listed. This outline can be presented on the chalkboard, overhead projector, or in a handout.

3. Use effective questioning techniques and discussions, as well as visual aids, charts, pictures, and graph organizers. If you allow members time to discuss a topic in small groups or with one other person, the persons with

learning disabilities will be better able to process the information with greater understanding. Individuals with learning disabilities appear to do better when they have many opportunities to verbalize what they are learning.

4. At the end of the discussion, summarize what was presented.

Using a common rule for public speaking is helpful when teaching individuals with learning disabilities: "Tell 'em what you're going to tell 'em; tell 'em; then tell 'em what you've told 'em." By providing opportunities for (1) previewing the main idea, (2) presenting the information in a well-organized approach using good questioning and discussion techniques, and then (3) summarizing the information presented, more opportunities for learning will occur. Other suggestions for your teaching include:

1. Before beginning the discussion, review the main concepts from last week and try to relate new information to old knowledge. By doing this, you will be integrating prior learning to new learning. This helps all learners acquire new information.

2. Provide practical problems that encourage the learner to apply concepts presented. Talk about them.

3. Rather than ask members to memorize Bible verses, ask for a paraphrase of the verse or discuss what the verse means.

4. Never ask class members to take turns reading the Bible passages aloud. Ask for volunteers, ask individuals in advance to read a selected passage, or read the passages aloud yourself.

5. Use mnemonic approaches when presenting new information. For example, an adult missionary with dyslexia used a mnemonic approach when he recently presented a talk to adults at our church. His topic was on the role of each individual as a missionary. The mnemonic approach was G-O-T. Step 1: Make God your number one priority in life. Step 2: Be Open to daily opportunities to serve God. Step 3: Take these opportunities to serve God and be a missionary. As do many adults with learning disabilities, this young man developed excellent compensatory strategies to assist him in remembering verbal sequences.

6. Provide members with videotapes and audiocassettes to supplement the printed material. For the individual who is motivated to study the material

in advance, tape record the printed material and offer this tape to the individual with a learning disability.

Your role as a teacher should be to help each person better understand of God's truth and to help each person live out this truth. If someone in your group has a learning disability, carefully consider the way you share God's love. Be appreciative that someone along the way has not alienated him or her from church. Remember that people with learning disabilities can have the same desire to learn and grow in their relationship with God as all others. They are just as intelligent and curious as everyone else is. They simply may need a different approach or added steps to their learning and growing process. These approaches may make you a more effective teacher to your entire class, too.

We may all need to recall the old Chinese proverb in our teaching: "I hear and I forget, I see and I remember, I do and I understand."

For further reading:

• *A Place for Everyone: A Guide for Special Education Bible Teaching-Reaching Ministry* by Athalene McNay (Nashville: Convention Press)

• *Teaching Adults: A Guide for Transformational Teaching* by Rick Edwards (Nashville: LifeWay Church Resources)

Adapted from an article written by Dr. Jane Hannah, assistant professor of pediatrics, Vanderbilt University Medical Center, Nashville, and a member of First Baptist Church, Nashville, Tennessee.

AdultApplication: **Do you have adults with special needs in your class? What techniques have you incorporated into your teaching to keep them involved and to help them learn? You may have adults with learning disabilities that you don't know about. How can new techniques help them? How might these same teaching-learning approaches help all learners?**

_____

_____

Adults and Faith

How would you draw a map of the faith development in adulthood? Would it show a flat terrain until death, or would there be hills and valleys along the way? Let's focus on some unique issues faced by adults as they travel through their spiritual journey.

While adults have many years to deepen and broaden their faith, the territory and direction of Christian growth in these years is hazy, especially if they have been in a strong youth program which emphasized discipleship and then move toward an adult program which is weak and inconsequential in contrast. Adults wonder if adult discipleship is just an adult version of the youth faith pilgrimage. Sometimes adults need to overcome poor or inadequate faith presentations learned as children or youth.

Read the following description of God from a young boy's perspective (written by Bruce Barton in the 1925 best-seller *The Man Nobody Knows*):

The little boy's body sat bolt upright in the rough wooden chair, but his mind was very busy.

This was his weekly hour of revolt.

The kindly lady who could never seem to find her glasses would have been terribly shocked if she had known what was going on inside the little boy's mind.

"You must love Jesus," she said every Sunday, "and God."

The little boy did not say anything. He was afraid to say anything; he was almost afraid that something would happen to him because of the things he thought:

Love God! Who was always picking on people for having a good time, and sending little boys to hell because they couldn't do better in a world he had made so hard! Why didn't God take on someone his own size?

Love Jesus! The little boy looked up at the picture, which hung on the Sunday-school wall. It showed a pale young man with flabby forearms and a sad expression. The young man had red whiskers.

Then the little boy looked across to the other wall. There was Daniel, good old Daniel, standing off the lions. The little boy liked Daniel. He liked David, too, with the trusty sling that landed a stone square on the forehead of Goliath. And Moses, with his rod and his big brass snake. They were winners—those three. He wondered if David could whip Jeffries. Samson could! Say, that would have been a fight!

But Jesus! Jesus was the "lamb of God." The little boy did not know what that meant, but it sounded like Mary's little lamb. Something for girls—sissified. Jesus was also "meek and lowly," a "man of sorrows and acquainted with grief." He went around for three years telling people not to do things.

Sunday was Jesus' day; it was wrong to feel comfortable or laugh on Sunday.

The little boy was glad when the superintendent thumped the bell and announced: "We will now sing the closing hymn." One more bad hour was over. For one more week the little boy had got rid of Jesus.

AdultApplication: **Reread that description of the little boy's faith. This time underline words and phrases that show immature faith. What challenges do adult leaders have when confronted by biblical and theological ignorance and illiteracy? What kinds of misunderstandings do your adult group members bring into the classroom?**

_____

_____

_____

With the provocative title *What Prevents Christian Adults from Learning?* John Hull has given a fresh diagnosis of the central problem of today's church, namely why adults have such a reluctance to be involved in church educational programs for them. According to Hull, adults are taught as children that the Christian faith is something one grows out of. It is necessary, yes, for children and youth, because they are in a learning mode most of their growing up years. That is, they are in school, and Sunday School is appropriate for them. So, when they become adults, over 18, they no longer need the trappings of youth or childhood. In fact, they define themselves as adults in part by not needing schooling anymore. These adults insist that children and youth need religious training but they do not.

More than likely you have heard strong support for calling a children's minister or a youth director but not a minister to adults. Part of this lack of attention to adult spiritual maturity can be traced to Hull's assumptions. "So it is that as adults and parents we socialize our children into that for which we have a fond nostalgia but can no longer take seriously ourselves. Deep in their hearts many adults believe that religion really is for children" (Hull, p. 8). Children and youth observe this as well. They conclude that if parents and other adults are not really committed to their own growing discipleship, they can "look forward" to the days when they can stop growing spiritually as well—as adults.

How then do Christian adults face their hypocrisy? In Christian education settings they often give the safe, remembered answers they learned as children. They seek to preserve, not enhance, the faith once delivered to them long ago. These adults pay a high price for their failure to go on growing in discipleship in their adult years. They have stopped learning. They know the church answers. They can recite the Sunday morning schedule for worship. They know the major Bible stories. They have "got it down," so to speak.

Ironically, though, these same adults who have "got religion down" continue to grow and mature in other areas of their lives. They marry, have offspring, take on a career, get involved in civic life, and shoulder a host of other responsibilities. In family life and work they solve problems, seek answers, continuously retrain and retool. Then suddenly a crisis appears—a daughter gets pregnant or a son decorates his body with earrings and tattoos and becomes a punk rocker. Anxious adults then harness all the resources they can muster, including their faith. This is the midlife crisis of faith, when they cannot solve the spiritual problems of adulthood with a faith they left 25 years ago at age 18.

What else keeps Christian adults from learning? In most classes adults want to preserve and enhance their self-respect and self-image. So they are careful not to admit that they don't know the answer to a question posed by the teacher. In this case ignorance breeds embarrassment. Their greatest fear is having their ignorance discovered. They are afraid of giving the wrong answers because they are supposed to have learned all this information years ago as a child or youth. This is not the case for children and youth. Why? Because the childhood and youth years are times of education and growth. It is understandable that they don't know biblical truth.

We may feel uncomfortable with the little boy's thoughts about his Sunday School experience. And we would hope that future lessons would correct his impressions. However, many adults retain these impressions well into adulthood. One cause is that they had become Sunday School dropouts and were not involved in Christian education during their youth years. Or they unconsciously pick up these childhood interpretations from society and bring them to the adult Bible class.

The task of the adult Christian education teacher is formidable—not only to teach the current lesson but at the same time to shore up the shortcomings of years of childhood (mis)education.

AdultApplication: Consider the class of adults you lead. Do you teach in a way that invites participation, or has lack of participation led you to do all the talking? Do you reward/affirm participation/questions/comments—even when they are clearly incorrect or immature? On a scale of 1 to 10, with academic study at one end and personal application at the other, where does your teaching fall? What evidences of immaturity do you see among your class members? How can you encourage

them to grow? What about church members who are not involved in Bible study? How can they be encouraged to attend and to participate?

_____

_____

_____

_____

_____

_____

_____

_____

_____

_____

_____

_____

Church Participation by Adults

Why do adults choose a church? How do they make their choices? The church researcher, George Barna, surveyed American adults with the following factors:

These are a few key factors that determine whether adults will return to a church they have visited. From the following 22 factors, rate them as extremely important, pretty important, somewhat important, not too important, or not at all important in your decision of whether to return to a church you have visited.

_____ Variety of programs

_____ Type of music

_____ How much you like the pastor

_____ Background of attendees

_____ Theological beliefs

_____ Quality of Adult Sunday School

_____ Denomination

_____ How much it emphasizes fund-raising

_____ Number of good friends

_____ Quality of sermons

_____ Convenience of meeting times

_____ Comfort of sanctuary

_____ Distance from home

_____ Availability of small groups

_____ How much people care

_____ Help to poor and disadvantaged

_____ Friendliness to visitors

_____ Quality of music

_____ Amount of music

_____ Length of music

Now, circle the factors over which you, a volunteer adult leader, have an influence.

For further reading:

• Stephen Arterburn and Jack Fulton, *Toxic Faith: Understanding and Overcoming Religious Addiction* (Nashville: Oliver Nelson, 1991).

• John Sisemore, *Church Growth Through the Sunday School* (Nashville: Broadman Press, 1983).

_____

Survey reported in *On Mission*, July-August 1999, 9.

AdultApplication: **Look at the items you checked and especially those you circled. Based on what attracts you to a church and keeps you there, how can you help meet others' needs? Do you think your reasons are unique or similar to others in your church? If items you have not marked may be important to others, how can you help make those positive factors in your church?**

_____

_____

_____

_____

_____

_____

_____

_____

Religious Cults and Adults

This past decade has seen an explosion of interest and involvement in religious cults in America and around the world. For instance, 39 members of the Heaven's Gate, including their founder Marshall Applewhite, committed mass suicide in an effort to shed their earthly containers and move to a higher level of experience aboard a spaceship they believed to be following the Hale-Bopp comet. Around the earth fundamentalists declare war on the unsuspecting. Rival political parties assume a religious aura and language.

Why then do adults join religious cults? An easy, but not definitive answer is that they want to; adults do what they want to do. They may not know why they are attracted to cults or give large sums of money and time to them, but they do. Maybe they are hoping the cult or its leaders can give them some sense of life.

But what is a cult? It is a religious group with a distinctive theological view that varies greatly from the dominant religion in a country or society. The usual structure is "us versus them." Hence, cults are often authoritarian in nature.

Adults join cults because they believe the leaders and the group can give meaning to their lives. They lack self-confidence.

These persons believe that they are victims of events and society over which they have no control. Or they may perceive themselves to be a part of a despised race or class.

Generally cults appeal to young adults, ages 18–28. Young adults are most attracted to cults at times of transitions in their lives—leaving home, deciding on a career, entering college or work, and getting married. When adults are in transition, especially when their own family is dysfunctional or far away, they find cults attractive because cults have definite beliefs and lifestyles. Maybe cult members provide them with the support and "family" lacking in their lives. People join cults not because they have discovered an intellectual destination but because they have found a social and psychological safety net.

Near the end of the Sermon the Mount, Jesus offered a stern warning against false prophets and teachers—then as well as now. Matthew 7:15-23 says:

Watch out for false prophets. They come to you in sheep's clothing, but inwardly they are ferocious wolves. By their fruit you will recognize them. Do people pick grapes from thornbushes, or figs from thistles? Likewise every good tree bears good fruit, but a bad tree bears bad fruit. A good tree cannot bear bad fruit, and a bad tree cannot bear good fruit. Every tree that does not bear good fruit is cut down and thrown into the fire. Thus, by their fruit you will recognize them. Not everyone who says to me, "Lord, Lord" will enter the kingdom of heaven, but only he who does the will of my Father who is in heaven. Many will say to me on that day, "Lord, Lord, did we not prophesy in Your name, and in your name drive out demons and perform many miracles?" Then I will tell them plainly, 'I never knew you. Away from me, evildoers!'"

AdultApplication: **What connections can you make between adults being caught up in childhood beliefs about church and/or Bible study and finding a cult inviting? How can you ensure that adults' needs are being met, particularly at times of transition, so that cults are not an option? List adult transitions. How does your church/class minister to adults at these times?**

_____

_____

_____

_____

_____

Physical Health and Adults

Every parent knows the importance of regular well-baby checkups. They help ensure the health of the infant and provide an essential foundation for health in the adult years. But in the midst of ensuring their children's health, those same adults may fail to follow a pattern of regular physical exams themselves. They fail to maintain their own health and well-being. Preventive care is the key to detecting health problems early and taking steps to treating them.

How is this relevant to understanding the adults with whom we work in the church? Sooner or later adults will face the inevitable physical signs of aging. For some the onset is bifocals; for others it is prostate or skin cancer. Others observe the physical decline of their parents and remember that their generation is the next to face these issues. Other adults fiercely resist any attempt to prevent or improve their physical condition by refusing to do monthly breast exams or have prostrate screening, exercising sporadically and becoming overweight. Each of these attitudes represents both learning and ministry opportunities. As Christian leaders plan sessions, they should remember that these represent actual needs of their members and discover ways to use the resources of the Christian faith to help these adults to know that God wants their best, not just spiritually, but physically as well.

I visited an Adult Sunday School class in a large metropolitan city. Most of the members were in their 30s and 40s. One of the customs of the class was to provide a prayer list for all members. Most of the prayer requests related to health concerns. Listen to their concerns: (I have changed the names.)

Paul had back surgery. He's still having some pain but is returning to work.

Fred's wife, Margie, has decided not to take any more chemo. Basically she has given up on life.

Wilma's body was not able to handle cancer treatments with the increased dosages.

In this class the predominant prayer thoughts focused on physical healing for themselves and their friends and relatives.

It goes without saying that Christian leaders should model good physical conditioning by maintaining a healthy weight, eating a nutritious diet, exercising regularly, protecting their skin from the sun, and getting plenty of rest. Pastors and other Christian leaders can also take additional steps to address health concerns of their adult members.

1. Provide helpful pamphlets and Internet addresses, which focus on health issues, faced by their members. The church library should be a good source for this information.

2. Evaluate the settings for churchwide events. How important is it to have daylong outdoor activities when all ages would be exposed to the sun?

3. Take a look at the menu for the Wednesday night meal and other meals offered by the church. What is the nutritional value of fried chicken, mashed potatoes, and coleslaw? Do you offer alternatives for those who are watching their diet?

4. Consider exercising programs for aging baby boomers. One church built a recreational facility for young families during the 70s, but because of the declining number of the church's young adults, the facility is largely unused during the week. Farsighted lay leaders saw the opportunity to make the facility available early in the morning for older middle-agers to walk around the tract and do aerobic exercises. A warm cup of coffee and cold orange juice are available to those who arrive early.

5. Consider adapting rooms for the growing aging population. One church realized that valuable first-floor space was unused. With a minimum of remodeling, they now have room to grow new Sunday School departments for the "young old" who make up a significant group in their church.

6. Present a positive view of the aging process. Many older persons face each day with vigor and zest. They attempt new challenges every day. Despite some physical limitations they engage in life. In short, old age is not for sissies!

7. Be alert to physical changes in people in your group. Sometimes these are revealed in prayer requests, but at other times they are too personal to be revealed to a group. For instance, Jay, 55, discovered that he had

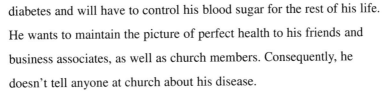

diabetes and will have to control his blood sugar for the rest of his life. He wants to maintain the picture of perfect health to his friends and business associates, as well as church members. Consequently, he doesn't tell anyone at church about his disease.

8. Take seriously the suggestions offered for air-conditioning and heating adaptations for older persons. As we age, our skin becomes thinner. Have you seen the hands of older persons? You can see the veins underneath their skin. Skin acts as a covering for the body, but it also provides insulation. As the room temperature drops, seniors feel the effects more quickly than younger adults do because their skin is thinner.

9. Finally, train church leaders, including deacons, to recognize and relate to the physical challenges of aging. Christian leaders should minister to the whole person, not just to spiritual needs. Ministering in Christ's name means serving the whole person.

Jay visited Mona in the nursing facility last week. Over the past two years, they have developed a strong personal relationship. As he entered the room, he noticed that her toenails needed clipping. With some apprehension he asked her if he could clip her toenails. As he bent down and began to clip her nails, he remembered the admonition of Jesus that "whatever you did for one of the least of these brothers of mine, you did for me" (Matt. 25:40). Both wept— she to receive this personal gift of ministry, and he to extend his gift of service.

For further study as well as group study, use the resource series *fit4 Wellness Plan* and *First Place Bible Study* (available by calling 1-800-458-2772).

AdultApplication: **How should the church recognize and respond to needs for healing? What other kinds of prayer requests should be shared besides physical ones? How can you encourage an expanded view of prayer needs in your class? Review the needs listed above. Add other needs evident in your church. How can your church respond?**

Understanding Today's Adults: 25 Years and Older

Understanding Today's Adults: 25 Years and Older

Grandparenting

Grandma. Gran. Grandad. Grandmother. Grandfather. Granny. Paw-Paw. Perhaps your favorite title for your grandparents is one of these. Most of us can remember some special term or characteristic of our grandparents. My "Granny" knew just how to get her grandchildren into a cool swimming pool in the middle of August or into bed at night. She just said her favorite warning, "Last one in is a rotten egg!" For most of us, grandparents are or were the anchor that holds a family together and provides a source of inspiration for all. Recently, however, new concerns in grandparenting began to emerge, such as grandparents' rights to see their grandchildren after the parents divorce and grandparents raising their own grandchildren.

A number of reasons have increased the number of grandparents raising their grandchildren, including the incarceration of parents, drug use, and the AIDS epidemic. It has been estimated that at the dawn of the 21st century 125,000 children will have lost their mothers because of AIDS. Often these children wind up in a grandparent's home. As may be expected, this new responsibility puts immediate economic strain on these older persons.

Church leaders can help these older persons by recognizing the special challenges they face. Grandparents who are raising grandchildren face problems with their own health and access to health care. Frequently they face depression and tend to delay seeking care for themselves, especially with emotional problems. As might be expected, they have fewer contacts with their friends, and their marital satisfaction declines.

Church leaders can improve the quality of life of grandparents who are raising grandchildren by offering support groups, which can offer important short-term emotional and informational provisions. AARP offers assistance through its Grandparent Information Center. They operate a computerized database of support groups and services.

Today's grandparents are in the midst of widespread dissolution and reconstruction of families, making kinship relationships more complicated. Researchers often speak of the "sandwich" generation, those who are simultaneously taking care of younger children and teens as well as older parents. These demands are often intense and competing. That is, these adults must make inevitable choices between caring for their children and their parents. Furthermore we are seeing the phenomenon of great-great grandchildren as the population ages, and 75 percent of adults can expect to become grandparents. Another indication of 21st-century changes in grandparenting is the emergence of adult grandchildren, whereas in earlier years the attention was on much younger grandchildren.

For further reading:

• *Grandparenting by Grace—LIFE Course* by Irene M. Endicott and C. Ferris Jordan (Nashville: Convention Press)

AdultApplication: **Does your church have grandparents who are caring for grandchildren part- or full-time? Some may be caring for grandchildren while parents work. Even this can be draining and confining for senior adults. How can your church support these grandparents and help to meet their needs?**

_____

_____

_____

_____

_____

_____

Race Issues in Adulthood

Racism expresses itself in many different ways, but it has served to undermine the essential unity of all God's creation, suggesting a superior and an inferior race. The Christian message concerning racial and ethnic diversity is clear: we are one in Christ. God asks, "What will you do with Jesus?" not, "What is your racial or ethnic background?" Did you know that there are more than three thousand African-American churches in the Southern Baptist Convention? Their annual growth rate of 13 percent annually exceeds all other groups in the SBC, including Hispanics. One in four Americans is a member of an ethnic minority.

God desires that everyone should recognize the essential relatedness of all persons. No one is above another; all stand together—women and men, young and old, disabled and healthy.

The key to building relationships among ethnic groups is understanding and respecting cultural differences. These differences occur in every facet of life. Gender roles in the family, attitudes toward work, worship styles, and language differences are approached with diverse perspectives among the races. A lack of respect and acceptance of this diversity causes churches to fail with attempts to reach many people groups.

Debra Berry, Woman's Missionary Union consultant, suggests a bridge builder for predominantly African-American congregations. Women on Mission "Sisters Who Care" is a strategy to strengthen the role of their missions organizations. The word *sister* resonates in the African-American community, where Christian women are sisters through their mutual faith in Christ, ethnic heritage, and as members of God's creation. You can order free resources for "Sisters Who Care" by calling 1-800-968-7301 or order online at *www.wmustore.com*.

How can believers in Jesus Christ work to recognize and eliminate racism in the church and the world? In a practical way, how can believers enhance reconciliation and become bridge builders? Mike Lundy, who works with the Baptist General Convention of Texas, suggests these ways:

- Stand up for Christian convictions about racial and ethnic reconciliation.
- Establish and maintain communications among nearby ethnic groups.
- Enrich fellowship among ethnic groups.

• Encourage pastors to preach on racial/ethnic reconciliation.

• Witness and minister to all racial groups.

• Establish partnerships with ethnically different congregations to do the work of Christ.

• Broaden the ethnic diversity of congregations.

AdultApplication: Does your church community have an unchurched ethnic group living within five miles of your building? If yes, how are these people different from your church members? What needs to be done to reach these people?

_____

_____

_____

_____

_____

_____

_____

Friendships in Adulthood

Georgia shifted nervously as she joined the congregation in singing "What a Friend We Have in Jesus." She was convinced that Jesus was her best friend. But as she scanned the audience, she thought, *Even though all these people are singing this song, I don't know anybody here. I could not single out anyone whom I would call my friend, even though I have a nodding acquaintance with dozens of them. What does it take to make friends here?* Many believers face Georgia's dilemma. What is friendship in adulthood? Can friendship exist between men and women, between men, and between women?

If you were to list the most significant people in your life, your list would certainly include friends. Friendships are formed on the basis of mutual feelings of affection, loyalty, and emotional disclosure.

For the most part we choose friends whom we see as like us in age, marital status, who live close to us, or with whom we have shared a momentous event together. We may have educational similarities or common interests or attitudes.

AdultApplication: What is your definition of a "good" friend? Think about your friends. Where and under what circumstances did you meet? How did your relationship move from acquaintance to friendship? How do you maintain your friendships? What threats have occurred to jeopardize your friendships?

_____

_____

There are decided advantages for adults to form friendships. Having an intimate friend has been shown to be related to higher morale and less depression, even during periods of major role losses such as a spouse's death.

Researchers are coming to acknowledge the critical roles played by informal relationships such as families, neighbors, and even acquaintances such as grocery clerks and letter carriers. They are especially important to adults as they age.

Older persons who have family members nearby may turn to friends and neighbors for immediate assistance before they turn to family members because friendships involve mutual and voluntary exchanges between equals. Such may not be the case between family members. The nature of the task at hand dictates whether family members, neighbors, or other friends are called upon. Friends are often the links between the elderly and community services among ethnic minorities. As persons age, they may be reluctant to move closer to their children and other family members because friends are an important source of companionship and losing friends in the senior years can be difficult. Although friendships decline from mortality, elders steadily make new friends from acquaintances and neighbors, and close relationships get closer with age.

Friendships vary according to gender. As may be expected, women have many more intimate friendships. For many men their wives are their only confidants. Losing one's spouse then is especially devastating. In contrast, women satisfy their needs for intimacy throughout their lives by developing close friendships. Therefore they are less emotionally dependent on their marital relationship when divorce or widowhood occurs. Men have large social networks, and when they interact, they are more likely to compete with one another and less likely to agree or support one another. In adulthood women disclose more, talk more. On the other hand men do things together rather than talk. They are more task than relationship oriented.

Both men and women choose friends from among the people they consider their social peers. They may be similar in age, sex, marital status, and social class. Because of this, parents are not likely to develop friendships with their children. Church leaders should recognize the need for these kinds of relationships and group adults in classes with their peers so they can begin and develop friendships. Peer friendships provide common ties based on shared life transitions and similar work experiences. Age as a basis for friendship becomes more important as the person's ties to other networks, such as work, are lessened.

Understanding Today's Adults: 25 Years and Older

This analysis of friendship patterns for adults has great consequences for church leaders of adults. Adults attend church activities week after week in part because they expect to see their friends. The common practice of prayer requests before Bible teaching is an expression of compassion for their friends and acquaintances. In addition, adults who volunteer to teach and serve enhance their sense of belonging to a group of friends. Beyond the church neighbors give mutual help as they solve problems together and exchange resources. Have you ever loaned a neighbor a rake or ladder? Neighbors are friends who live near us.

AdultApplication: List the names of your friends. Are you satisfied with the number of your friends? Are you satisfied with the quality of your friendships? In your church are members of adult groups friends? Are events planned to encourage friendships? If members are already good friends, are newcomers welcome?

_____

_____

_____

Social Convoys

Whether naturally or by design, adults fall into social convoys as they age. These divisions may be by age, generation, or marital status. Older, unmarried women in a church may form an informal group and go out to eat each Sunday afternoon. Families whose sons and daughters are playing soccer form friendships based on their children's activities. Women and men form friendships at work that endure over decades. In many churches a group of widows sit every week on the same row, identifying themselves as a friendship group.

The word *mentor* has made its way into our vocabulary in the past two decades. It is a distinctive form of friendship. In popular terminology a mentor is a person, usually older and more experienced, who is able and willing to help a protégé where he or she wants to go. The usual scheme is for the mentor to fix the road ahead and give the novice traveler a map. However, in the Christian context mentors are trusted guides into life, rather than a tour director, more interested in developing competent travelers along the adult journey.

In fact, we can make a strong case for mentoring as a new form of teaching and learning with adults. Adults learn through highly attentive observation of another person's behavior. Mentors provide support, challenge, and vision to others. Support is extended when we affirm their experiences. We understand. Challenge is the second feature of mentorship. Support brings them to us, and challenge peels them apart. Challenge opens up a gap that creates tension. Mentors deliberately set high standards and have high expectations of their students. In short, they challenge to challenge themselves.

For further reading:

• *Woman to Woman: Preparing Yourself to Mentor* by Edna Ellison and Tricia Scribner (Birmingham: New Hope Press)

• *Woman to Woman: How to Start, Grow, and Maintain a Mentoring Ministry* by Janet Thompson (Nashville: LifeWay Church Resources)

• *Drawing Men to God: Men's Ministry Manual* by Sid Woodruff (Nashville: LifeWay Church Resources)

AdultApplication: In what way did Jesus establish a mentor relationship with His disciples?

_____

_____

_____

_____

Group Study Guide

Purpose: To provide teachers and leaders of adults with the opportunity to reflect on what they read in this resource, talk with one another, and apply the information to the adults in their groups.

Objective: Through reflection and conversation teachers and leaders will develop an understanding of the adults in their groups. With this understanding they will be able to transform their methods to match the needs and characteristics of their adult learners.

Participants: This plan is for teachers, leaders, and ministers who relate to adults, 25 years and older.

Sessions: This plan can be used in a variety of settings including retreats, planning meetings, and conferences. Suggestions are designed for one-hour sessions, but you are encouraged to adapt it to meet the needs of your group. For example, you can easily adjust the suggestions to fit a 15-minute training segment during a planning meeting. Also, feel free to use the reflection exercises in any order. A conclusion exercise to the entire study is located at the end of the session titled "Adults and Life Issues." Use this exercise at the end of your last session.

Approach: This plan is designed for a group of teachers and leaders to participate in a discussion based on what they have read in this resource. The convener serves as facilitator of the discussion. Group members participate by sharing their reflections or thoughts concerning what they have read. The exercises enable participants to identify implications for applying the information to their adult learners.

Room arrangement: Having tables and chairs arranged in a square is preferable so that participants can see one another. If tables are not available, arrange chairs in a circle.

Session: Introduction

Preparation

- Print class rolls for teachers or gather paper and pencils.
- Order copies of *Understanding Today's Adults: 25 Years and Older* (allow three weeks for delivery) or download the contents page and make copies.
- Provide name tags if participants do not know one another.

Reflect and Practice

1. As participants arrive, distribute the class rolls or ask them to write down the names of the adults in their class or group. Guide them to keep this list with them during group discussions so they can consider how the information is true of the individuals in their groups.

2. Distribute copies of this book or the contents page to participants. Ask participants to share what they would like to learn about the adults in their groups. Refer them to the contents page. As a group, determine the order of sections the group will discuss.

3. Encourage the members of your group to read before each session the section to be discussed during the session. The group experience will be enhanced by individuals reading the section to prepare for the discussion. Have a season of prayer to give each person an opportunity to make a commitment to understand the adults in his or her group.

4. Depending on which section your group decided to discuss first, ask them to share what they know about the subject and what they want to learn during the next session. For example, if your group decided to reflect on the section "Adults and Learning," ask them to share a learning experience in their own lives that changed their behavior. Ask, "What do you want to learn about learning as we read this week and reflect next time?"

5. Close the session with a prayer concerning personal needs and concerns of participants. Remind participants to read the section for the next session.

Session: Today's Adults

Preparation

• Look through the comic strips in newspapers and magazines to find funny illustrations that answer the question, what does it mean to be an adult? Cut them out and prepare them for sharing with your participants.

• Ask your pastor or a staff person to let you borrow a copy of demographic studies for your church community. Prepare a summary of information from the report with implications for adults. If your church does not have such a study, assist your pastor or staff person in getting one from your Baptist state convention office (ask for the Scan US office).

Reflect and Practice

1. As participants arrive, share the comic strips with them.

2. Open the discussion with prayer.

3. Ask, "How does the concept of maturity fit your group of adults?" (See p. 10.) After a brief discussion, ask, "As a teacher or leader, what can you do to foster growth in the maturity of your learners?"

4. Distribute copies of the summary of the demographic study of your church community. Ask, "What implications do you see for our adult classes and groups?" Continue the discussion about what your study group could do to help your church respond to the church community. For example, did you find a nearby ethnic group that needs a church family? Did you find that your community has a significant number of single adults?

5. Take a few minutes for the group to identify experiences in their lives that have influenced their personal mental, physical, emotional, and spiritual development. Refer to pages 19–20 as a discussion starter. Ask, "How have these experiences affected your own development?" Discuss ways of discovering developmental issues in the lives of people in their classes or groups.

6. Conclude this session by making a list of implications for teachers and leaders to consider for their classes or groups as a result of this session.

7. Close in prayer. Remind participants to read the section for the next session.

Session: The Middle Adult Years

Preparation

• If teachers and leaders in your group only relate to senior adults, skip this section.

• Enlist a panel of guests to meet with your group to include a married couple experiencing the empty nest syndrome, a single parent, and a person who has experienced career difficulties (unemployment or underemployment).

Reflect and Practice

1. Open the discussion with prayer.

2. Ask group members to study their list of names of people in their class or group. Write a word or phrase beside each name to describe his or her situation. Use the list of life events on page 27 under "The Real Middle Adult" as a discussion starter. Discuss how Bible study, mission study, discipleship, and mentoring groups can comfort and guide the men and women through their circumstances.

3. Introduce your special guests. Interview each person with the following questions.

   With the "post-parental" couple ask, "How did you individually respond to your child's leaving home? How has your child's departure affected your marriage? How can our church family minister to you?" Let your participants dialogue with the couple

   Ask the single parent to share concerns and issues that complicate his or her life. "How has our church family assisted you with these concerns and issues? What can our church family do now to minister with you and other single parents?" Invite participants to talk with the single parent.

   Ask the fourth panel member to share his or her experiences with unemployment or underemployment. "What are specific ways our church family can help with unemployment and underemployment? How can we minister to your family?" Open the discussion for the entire group to reflect on unemployment and underemployment.

4. With the panel compile a list of common needs mentioned by the guests that could be met by your church family. Ask teachers and leaders to reflect on their current ministry actions and to identify what they could do in the near future. Be sure to thank your special guests as they leave.

5. Close the session with a season of prayer for the middle adults in your church. Remind participants to read the section for the next session.

Session: The Senior Adult Years

Preparation

• If teachers and leaders in your group only relate to middle adults, skip this section.

• Prepare a printout or summary of the current statistics of middle adults in your church. This information will be used in considering how many persons will become senior adults in the next five years. Duplicate as a handout or write the information on the marker board.

Reflect and Practice

1. Open the session with fellowship and prayer.

2. Ask, "How does our church family consider senior adults?" Let the group openly reflect on ways your church values or fails to value senior adults.

3. As a group, review the quiz on pages 42–44. Discuss any surprises to the group.

4. Reflect on the disengagement and activity approaches to aging (46–47). Identify church actions that indicate disengagement on the part of your church. Discuss ways teachers and leaders of senior adults can advocate for the needs and participation of senior adults.

5. Distribute the statistics on middle adults in your church, or point the group toward the marker board. Ask your group to reflect on the number of persons who will be retiring or becoming senior adults in the next five years. Ask, "How will these new senior adults affect our senior adult ministry? What can

we do now to minister to new retirees?"

6. Ask participants to divide into five groups. Let each group select one of the "Aging Adult Groups" on page 51. Ask the groups to evaluate the senior adults in your church who are in these groups. Are the concerns on pages 49–50 true for your senior adults? How do they differ? Ask each subgroup to report their conclusions to the whole group.

7. As a group, list the names of persons who are caring for aging parents in your church. Ask, "How can we learn more about caregivers and their needs in our church?" Let the group be creative in developing a strategy. Encourage them to do something with the strategy. These actions will take place beyond your group sessions.

8. Close the session with a season of prayer for senior adults and caregivers. Remind your participants to read the section for the next session.

Session: Adults and Learning

Preparation
• Ask teachers to bring their teaching guides to this session.

Reflect and Practice

1. Open the session with prayer.

2. Ask, "How do you see your group of adults experiencing learning: a calling or a journey?" (pp. 56–57)

3. Ask participants to pair off. With their partners ask them to identify how to use reflection in the next lesson or session with their learners. You are asking them to reflect on what they read in the article "Adults and Learning" then practice the art of reflection during the next session with their adult learners. If you have general church leaders in your group, discuss ways to use reflection in their leadership meetings.

4. As a group, identify tips for using reflection opportunities with their adult learners. Some of their tips may come from their experiences with this study.

5. Ask your participants to review their list of group members. Say, "Analyze your experiences with each person. Do any of his or her behaviors indicate a learning disability?" As a group, discuss the strategy and organizational instruction approach on pages 63–65. Ask, "How does this approach complement reflection?"

6. Conclude the session by discussing the implications of how adults learn to the ways teachers teach and lead adults. Ask, "How can you create an environment where adults expect to learn something when they come to church?"

7. Close the session with prayer asking God to guide the teachers and leaders to focus on learning more than teaching. Remind your participants to read the section for the next session.

Session: Adults and Spiritual Growth

Preparation
• Gather sheets of paper (8½ by 14) and pencils.

Reflect and Practice
1. Open the session with prayer.

2. Distribute the paper and pencils. Ask your participants to write their spiritual growth time lines on the sheets of paper before this session. Ask them to mark the time line with their faith development milestones.

3. Spend this session letting each participant share his or her time line. As they listen, compile a list of common elements in the way participants have grown spiritually. Ask, "How do our experiences compare to those described on pages 66–67?"

4. As a group, consider ways to evaluate the spiritual growth of the adults in their classes and groups. Ask, "Is the amount of church participation a sign of spiritual growth?"

5. Ask your participants to reflect on the influence of religious cults and the adults in their classes and groups (p. 73). Identify the life transitions being

Understanding Today's Adults: 25 Years and Older

experienced by adults in their groups. Ask, "How can you help them through these transitions so that they will not be tempted by cults?"

6. Close the session by praying for specific adults experiencing transitions. Remind your participants to read the section for the next session.

Session: Adults and Life Issues

Preparation
• Gather four shoe boxes and materials such as several recent newspapers and magazines, glue sticks, markers, and scissors.
• Place one shoe box with materials in each corner of the room.
• Assign each area one of the life issues: Physical Health, Grandparenting, Race Issues, and Friendships.

Reflect and Practice
1. Open the session with prayer.
2. Ask participants to be creative during this session. Say, "Select an issue in one of the corners of our room. Go to that area and start working on a collage dealing with that issue. Cut out pictures and key words that illustrate the implications of the issue and effective ways to deal with that issue. Glue them to the box. Prepare two questions to lead our group in a time of reflection on your issue."
3. Let the participants work in their groups. At the appropriate time ask them to come back together and begin the presentations/reflections.
4. Conclude the session by identifying ways teachers and leaders can minister to people in their groups regarding these issues. Ask, "What can our study group do to influence our church leaders to respond to these issues in our church and community?"
5. If this is your last session, spend a few moments reflecting on the experiences your participants have had with this study. Ask, "What difference has this experience had on the way you teach and minister? What actions can we

take to encourage our church family to be more intentional in ministering to adults?"

6. Close with a concert of prayer where teachers and leaders verbalize the names of adults in their groups at the same time. Open the prayer time for specific requests and concerns about understanding adults in your church and community.

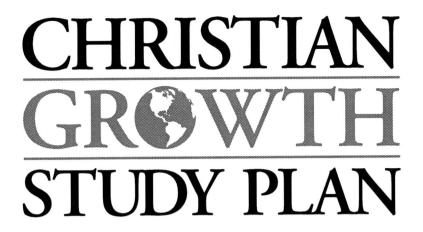

CHRISTIAN GROWTH STUDY PLAN

In the **Christian Growth Study Plan (formerly Church Study Course),** this book *Understanding Today's Adults 25 Years and Older* is a resource for course credit in six Leadership and Skill Development diploma plans. To receive credit, read the book, complete the learning activities, show your work to your pastor, a staff member or church leader, then complete the following information. This page may be duplicated. Send the completed page to:

**Christian Growth Study Plan
127 Ninth Avenue, North, MSN 117
Nashville, TN 37234-0117
FAX: (615)251-5067**

For information about the Christian Growth Study Plan, refer to the current Christian Growth Study Plan Catalog. Your church office may have a copy. If not, request a free copy from the Christian Growth Study Plan office (615/251-2525).

COURSE CREDIT INFORMATION

Please check the appropriate box indicating the diploma you want to apply this credit. You may check more than one.

❑ Leadership Skill Development (LS-0002)

❑ Adult Leadership Sunday School (LS-0035)

❑ Adult Leadership Discipleship Training (LS-0035)

❑ Adult Leadership Adults on Mission (LS-0035)

❑ Adult Leadership Women on Mission (LS-0035)

❑ Adult Leadership Senior Adult Ministry (LS-0035)

PARTICIPANT INFORMATION

Rev. 6-99

Social Security Number (USA Only)	Personal CGSP Number*	Date of Birth (Mo., Day, Yr.)
Name (First, MI, Last)		Home Phone
Address (Street, Route, or P.O. Box)	City, State, or Province	Zip/Postal Code

CHURCH INFORMATION

Church Name		
Address (Street, Route, or P.O. Box)	City, State, or Province	Zip/Postal Code

CHANGE REQUEST ONLY

❑Former Name		
❑Former Address	City, State, or Province	Zip/Postal Code
❑Former Church	City, State, or Province	Zip/Postal Code
Signature of Pastor, Conference Leader, or Other Church Leader		Date

*New participants are requested but not required to give SS# and date of birth. Existing participants, please give CGSP# when using SS# for the first time. Thereafter, only one ID# is required. *Mail To:* Christian Growth Study Plan, 127 Ninth Ave., North, MSN 117, Nashville, TN 37234-0117. Fax: (615)251-5067